History Summarized

ARAB–ISRAELI CONFLICT

WORLD
BOOK

www.worldbook.com

World Book, Inc.
180 North LaSalle Street
Suite 900
Chicago, Illinois 60601
USA

For information about other "History Summarized" titles, as well as other World Book print and digital publications, please go to **www.worldbook.com**.

For information about other World Book publications, call 1-800-WORLDBK (967-5325).

For information about sales to schools and libraries, call 1-800-975-3250 (United States) or 1-800-837-5365 (Canada).

Library of Congress Cataloging-in-Publication Data for this volume has been applied for.

History Summarized
ISBN: 978-0-7166-3800-1 (set)

Arab-Israeli Conflict
978-0-7166-3801-8 (hc.)

Also available as:
ISBN: 978-0-7166-3811-7 (e-book)

Printed in China by Shenzhen Wing King Tong Paper Products Co., Ltd., Shenzhen, Guangdong
1st printing July 2018

STAFF

Writer: Tom Firme

Executive Committee

President
Jim O'Rourke

Vice President and
Editor in Chief
Paul A. Kobasa

Vice President, Finance
Donald D. Keller

Vice President, Marketing
Jean Lin

Vice President, International
Maksim Rutenberg

Vice President, Technology
Jason Dole

Director, Human Resources
Bev Ecker

Editorial

Director, New Print
Tom Evans

Manager
Jeff De La Rosa

Editor
Mellonee Carrigan

Librarian
S. Thomas Richardson

Manager, Contracts and
Compliance
(Rights and Permissions)
Loranne K. Shields

Manager, Indexing Services
David Pofelski

Digital

Director, Digital Product
Development
Erika Meller

Digital Product Manager
Jonathan Wills

Manufacturing/Production

Manufacturing Manager
Anne Fritzinger

Production Specialist
Curley Hunter

Proofreader
Nathalie Strassheim

Graphics and Design

Senior Art Director
Tom Evans

Coordinator, Design
Development and Production
Brenda Tropinski

Senior Visual
Communications Designer
Melanie Bender

Senior Designer
Isaiah Sheppard

Media Editor
Rosalia Bledsoe

Senior Cartographer
John M. Rejba

TABLE OF CONTENTS

"History Summarized"

Each book in this series concisely surveys a major historical event or interrelated series of events or a major cultural, economic, political, or social movement. Especially important and interesting aspects of the subject of each book are highlighted in feature sections. Use a "History Summarized" book as an introduction to its subject in preparation for deeper study or as a review of the subject to reinforce what has been studied about the topic.

What is the Arab-Israeli conflict?

The Arab-Israeli conflict is a struggle between the Jewish state of Israel and the Arabs of the Middle East. About 90 percent of all Arabs are Muslims. The conflict has included several wars between Israel and certain Arab countries that have opposed Israel's existence. Israel was formed in 1948. The conflict has also involved a struggle by Palestinian Arabs to establish their own country in some or all of the land occupied by Israel.

The Arab-Israeli conflict is the continuation of an Arab-Jewish struggle that began in the early 1900's for control of Palestine (*PAL uh styn*). Palestine today consists of Israel and the areas known as the Gaza (*GAH zuh*) Strip and the West Bank. The Gaza Strip is a territory on the eastern Mediterranean coast, where Egypt and Israel meet. It covers 141 square miles (365 square kilometers) and holds a population of about 2,020,000. The Gaza Strip is one of the most densely populated places in the world. The West Bank is a territory in the Middle East that lies between Israel and Jordan. It covers 2,263 square miles (5,860 square kilometers) and holds a population of about 2,850,000. The Arab people known as the Palestinians lived in the region long before Jews began moving there in large numbers in the late 1800's.

The Arab-Israeli conflict has been hard to resolve. In 1979, Egypt became the first Arab country to sign a peace treaty with Israel. Jordan, another Arab country, signed a peace treaty with Israel in 1994. But Israel has not made final peace agreements with Syria or with the Palestine Liberation Organization (PLO). The PLO is a political body that represents the Palestinian people.

In the late 1800's, some European Jews formed a movement to establish a Jewish state in Palestine. Jewish immigrants began arriving in Palestine in large numbers. This image shows Jewish refugees who were forced off the refugee ship **Exodus 1947** *(in the background)*, which tried to run thousands of Holocaust survivors past the British blockade of Palestine in 1947.

CHAPTER ONE

Background of the conflict; history of Palestine and Zionism

In the mid-1800's, Jewish intellectuals in Europe began to support the idea that Jews should settle in Palestine, which the Bible describes as the Jews' ancient homeland. The word *Palestine* does not appear in the Bible. But it has long been used to refer to the area the Bible describes. The idea that Jews should settle in Palestine became known as Zionism. In the 1800's, Palestine was controlled by the Ottoman Empire, which was centered in the present-day country of Turkey.

Zionism became an important political movement among Jews in Europe because of increasing *anti-Semitism* (prejudice against Jews) in Europe. Anti-Semitism resulted in violent attacks on Jews and their property. It included *pogroms* (riots against the Jews) in Russia.

Zionists revived the Jewish culture, and Modern Hebrew as the official and spoken language of the Jewish people. Zionists established the political and social institutions needed to re-create national Jewish life. Zionism now supports various projects in Israel and acts as a cultural bridge between Israel and Jews in other countries. *Zion* is the poetic Hebrew name for Palestine.

Groups of Jewish youths calling themselves *Hoveve-Zion* (Lovers of Zion) formed a movement in 1882 to promote immigration to Palestine. They started what was called *practical Zionism,* which established Jewish settlements in Palestine. Theodor Herzl (*TAY aw dohr HEHR tsuhl*) (1860-1904), an Austrian journalist, developed *political Zionism,*

Austrian journalist Theodor Herzl (left) organized the Zionist movement, which worked for political recognition of the historic region of Palestine as the homeland of the Jewish people. He believed the solution to anti-Semitism was the creation of a Jewish state. Herzl is shown above with his mother, Jeanette, around the 1890's.

which worked for political recognition of the Jewish claim to a Palestine homeland.

Herzl was a reporter at the famous trial in 1894 of Alfred Dreyfus. Dreyfus was a Jewish officer in the French army who was falsely convicted of treason. The Dreyfus affair convinced Herzl that if anti-Semitism could be an active force in a country as enlightened as France, Jews could not fit into non-Jewish society. To him, the only solution was to create an independent Jewish state.

Herzl organized the Zionist movement on a worldwide scale at the First Zionist Congress in Basel, Switzerland, in 1897. However, in the early 1900's, many Jews opposed the new movement. They included the extremely religious and those who sought full *assimilation*—that is, absorption into non-Jewish society.

In the 1800's, the immigration of European Jews to Palestine accelerated. At first, many of the immigrants and the Palestinians lived together peacefully. But as more Jews arrived, conflicts between the two groups increased.

Palestinians are an ethnic and national group native to the historic region of Palestine that now consists of Israel, the West Bank, and the Gaza Strip. Today, there are about 12.5 million Palestinians. About 60 percent now live outside what was Palestine—in nearby Arab countries and elsewhere. Most of these Palestinians are refugees or the descendants of the more than 700,000 refugees who fled or were driven out of Israel when the nation was created in 1948. Some are people who were forced to leave the Gaza Strip and the West Bank, which were occupied by Israel in 1967. Today, though some Palestinians still live in refugee camps, most have integrated socially and economically within the host countries. They hold a variety of professional positions and are an important part of the economies of several Middle Eastern countries.

Modern Palestinians claim to be descendants of the Philistines (*FIHL uh steenz* or *fuh LIHS tihnz*), an ancient people who settled the region near the end of the 1200's B.C., and other groups who arrived later. Arab culture became a dominant influence beginning about A.D. 638, when Muslim Arabs conquered much of the region. Palestinians today speak Arabic with regional accents that distinguish them from other Arab groups. Nearly all Palestinians are Muslims, with a large Christian minority.

The Palestinian people began to develop a modern national identity around 1900. Palestinian national identity has several sources. It comes in part from the religious attachment of Muslims and Christians to Palestine as a holy land. Palestinian nationalism and the desire for self-determination also developed as a response to Zionism.

In 1947, the UN voted to partition Palestine into a Jewish state and an Arab state and to place the city of Jerusalem (*juh ROO sul luhm*) under international control. The Jews in Palestine accepted this plan, but the Arabs rejected it. Israel came into existence in 1948. War immediately broke out between Israel and the surrounding Arab countries. Both the Arab and Jewish inhabitants of Palestine fought for control of the territory. By 1949, Israel had defeated the Arabs and gained control of about half the land planned for the new Arab state. The nations of Egypt and Jordan held the rest of Palestine. These areas came under Israeli control in 1967. Many of Palestine's residents became refugees.

Early history and settlement

The Middle East, also called the Near East, is a region made up of the lands of southwestern Asia and northeastern Africa. All definitions of the region include the countries of Bahrain, Egypt, Iran, Iraq, Israel, Jordan, Kuwait, Lebanon, Oman, Qatar, Saudi Arabia, Syria, Turkey, the United Arab Emirates, and Yemen. The definitions also include Palestine—the West Bank, the Gaza Strip, and Israel. Here, the term *Middle East* refers to these 15 countries and 2 territories. They cover about 2,812,000 square miles (7,283,000 square kilometers) and together have about 423 million people.

Some definitions of the Middle East include more countries. Afghanistan, Algeria, Cyprus, Libya, Morocco, Pakistan, Sudan, and Tunisia are the countries most often added.

About 2 million Palestinians are citizens of Jordan, while many others carry passports from the Palestinian Authority (PA). The Palestinian

The future of Jerusalem remains one of the most complex and delicate issues in the Arab-Israeli conflict. The Jaffa Gate (part of which is shown above in 1894) opens into the walls that enclose Jerusalem's Old City.

Authority is the political body that administers Palestinian-controlled portions of the Gaza Strip and West Bank. About 1 million Palestinians are citizens of Israel, where they have been subject to legal restrictions and often face discrimination. Many Palestinians in Lebanon, Syria, and Egypt remain stateless refugees with no citizenship.

Two great religions—Judaism and Christianity—originated in Palestine. It is the Holy Land, the site of many events described in the Bible. Muslims, the followers of the Islamic religion, also consider Palestine a sacred place.

Palestine's location between Egypt and southwest Asia has made it a center of conflict for thousands of years. Many peoples have invaded and taken control of the region.

Amorites (*AM uh ryts*), Canaanites (*KAY nuh nyts*), and other Semitic (*suh MIHT ihk*) peoples entered the area about 2000 B.C. The area became known as the Land of Canaan. Sometime between about 1800 and 1500 B.C., a Semitic people called Hebrews left the region known as Mesopotamia (*mehs uh puh TAY mee uh*) and settled in Canaan, where they became known as Israelites (*IHZ ree uh lyts*). Some of these Israelites later went to Egypt.

In the 1200's B.C., Moses led the Israelites out of Egypt, and they returned to Canaan. The Israelites practiced a religion centered on belief in one God. Other peoples in Canaan worshiped many gods.

For about 200 years, the Israelites fought the other peoples of Canaan

Sometime between 1800 and 1500 B.C., a Semitic people called Hebrews settled in the land of Canaan, where they became known as Israelites. For about 200 years, the Israelites fought the other peoples of Canaan. The Book of Joshua in the Hebrew Bible describes their conquest of Canaan. Canaan was later called Palestine.

and the neighboring areas. One of their strongest enemies, the Philistines, controlled the southwestern coast of Canaan—called Philistia.

Until about 1029 B.C., the Israelites were loosely organized into 12 tribes. The constant warfare with neighboring peoples led the Israelites to choose a king, Saul, as their leader. Saul's successor, David, unified the nation to form the Kingdom of Israel, about 1000 B.C. David established his capital in Jerusalem. His son, Solomon, succeeded him as king and built the first Temple for the worship of God. Israel remained united until Solomon's death about 928 B.C. The northern tribes of Israel then split away from the tribes in the south. The northern state continued to be called Israel. The southern state, called Judah (*JOO duh*), kept Jerusalem as its capital. The word *Jew,* which came to be used for all Israelites, comes from the name *Judah.*

Invasions and conquests

During the 700's B.C., the Assyrians (*uh SIHR ee uhnz*), a people who lived in what is now the country of Iraq, extended their rule westward to the Mediterranean Sea. They conquered Israel in 722 or 721 B.C. After about 100 years, the Babylonians (*bab uh LOH nee uhnz*) began to take over the Assyrian Empire. They conquered Judah in 587 or 586 B.C. and destroyed Solomon's Temple in Jerusalem. They enslaved many Jews and forced them to live in exile in Babylonia. About 50 years later, the Persian king Cyrus (*SY ruhs*) the Great (?-530 B.C.) conquered Babylonia. Cyrus allowed a group of Jews from Babylonia to rebuild and settle in Jerusalem.

The Persians ruled most of the Middle East, including Palestine, from about 530 to 331 B.C. Alexander the Great then conquered the Persian Empire. After Alexander's death in 323 B.C., his generals divided his empire. One of these generals, Seleucus (*suh LOO kuhs*) (358-281 B.C.), founded a *dynasty* (series of rulers) that gained control of much of Palestine about 200 B.C. At first, the new rulers, called Seleucids (*suh LOO sihdz*), allowed the practice of Judaism. But later, one of the kings, Antiochus (*an TY uh kuhs*) IV (215?-164 B.C.), tried to prohibit it. In 167 B.C., the Jews revolted under the leadership of Judah Maccabee (*JOO duh MAK uh bee*) (also spelled Judas Maccabaeus) and drove the Seleucids out of Palestine. The Jews reestablished an independent kingdom called Judah.

In 63 B.C., Roman troops invaded Judah, and it came under Roman control. The Romans called the area Judea (*joo DEE uh*). Jesus Christ was born in Bethlehem in the early years of Roman rule. Roman rulers put down Jewish revolts in A.D. 66 and A.D. 132. In A.D. 135, the Romans drove the Jews out of Jerusalem. The Romans named the area Palaestina, for Philistia, at about this time. The name *Palaestina* became *Palestine* in English.

Most of the Jews fled from Palestine. But Jewish communities continued to exist in Galilee (*GAL uh lee*), the northernmost part of Palestine. Palestine was governed by the Roman Empire until the A.D. 300's and then by the Byzantine Empire. In time, Christianity spread to most of Palestine.

During the A.D. 600's, Muslim Arab armies moved north from Arabia to conquer most of the Middle East, including Palestine. Muslim powers controlled the region until the early 1900's. The rulers allowed Christians and Jews to keep their religions. However, most of the population gradually accepted Islam and the Arab-Islamic culture of their rulers.

In the 1000's, the Seljuks (*sehl JOOKS*), a Turkish people, began to take over Palestine. They gained control of Jerusalem in 1071. Seljuk rule of Palestine lasted less than 30 years. Christian crusaders from Europe wanted to regain the land where their religion began. The Crusades

This painting shows the fall of the ancient kingdom of Tripoli (part of modern-day Lebanon) to the Egyptian-based Mamluks in 1289. The Mamluks established an empire in the region in the mid-1200's that in time included Palestine. Jews from Spain and other Mediterranean lands eventually settled in Jerusalem and other parts of Palestine.

started in 1096. The Christians captured Jerusalem in 1099. They held the city until 1187, when the Muslim ruler Saladin (*SAL uh dihn*) (1138-1193) attacked Palestine and took control of Jerusalem.

In the mid-1200's, Mamluks (*MAM looks*), also spelled Mamelukes, based in Egypt, established an empire that in time included Palestine. Arab Muslims made up most of Palestine's population. Beginning in the late 1300's, Jews from Spain and other Mediterranean lands settled in Jerusalem and other parts of Palestine. The Ottoman Empire defeated the Mamluks in 1516, and Palestine became part of the Ottoman Empire. The Jewish population slowly increased, and by 1880, about 24,000 Jews were living in Palestine.

Balfour Declaration

In 1917, British Foreign Secretary Arthur James Balfour (1848-1930) issued a British government document that dealt with the establishment of a Jewish homeland in Palestine. It was called the Balfour Declaration. In it, the United Kingdom supported creating a national homeland for the Jews. The document was interpreted differently by Arabs and Jews, who both claimed Palestine. It led to a bitter controversy that set the stage for continuing conflicts between Arabs and Israelis in the Middle East.

The Balfour Declaration read as follows: "His Majesty's Government view with favour the establishment in Palestine of a national home for the Jewish people, and will use their best endeavors to facilitate the achievement of this object, it being clearly understood that nothing shall be done which may prejudice the civil and religious rights of existing non-Jewish communities in Palestine, or the rights and political status enjoyed by Jews in any other country."

When the Balfour Declaration was issued, during World War I, British forces were fighting to win Palestine from the Ottoman Empire. The United Kingdom wanted to control Palestine because of its location near the Suez (*soo EHZ*) Canal, which links the Mediterranean Sea and the Red Sea. The British believed the Balfour Declaration would help gain support of this goal from Jewish leaders in the United Kingdom, the United States, and other countries. In 1918, at the end of World War I, the United Kingdom gained control of Palestine from the Ottoman Empire. In 1920, the League of Nations granted the United Kingdom a provisional *mandate* (order to rule) over Palestine. In 1922, the League

British Foreign Secretary Arthur James Balfour (right) issued the Balfour Declaration in 1917. The document supported making Palestine a national homeland for the Jews. The United Kingdom gained control of Palestine from the Ottoman Empire in 1918, at the end of World War I. Under British rule, the Jewish population in Palestine continued to grow.

endorsed the Balfour Declaration and officially approved the terms of the mandate.

Jews who supported the establishment of a Jewish national homeland in Palestine believed the Balfour Declaration pledged the United Kingdom's support for their goal. But leaders of a growing Arab nationalism movement in Palestine claimed the declaration allowed for such a homeland only if Arabs agreed to it.

Severe fighting broke out several times in the 1920's and 1930's due to disputes between Arabs and Jews because of differing views of the Balfour Declaration. Based on earlier British promises to them, Arab leaders assumed Palestine would be an Arab state. They demanded an

Chaim Weizmann

Chaim Weizmann (*KY ihm VYTS mahn* or *WYTS muhn*) (1874-1952) served as the first president of Israel from 1949 until his death on Nov. 9, 1952. From 1920 to 1930 and from 1935 to 1946, Weizmann was president of the World Zionist Organization. This organization worked to establish a national homeland in Palestine for the Jewish people. Weizmann headed the Jewish delegation to the Paris Peace Conference in 1919 and worked there to have the  League of Nations assign administration of Palestine to the United Kingdom. In 1917, the United Kingdom had issued the Balfour Declaration, which supported the idea of a Jewish national homeland in Palestine. His nephew Ezer Weizman (1924-2005) was president of Israel from 1993 to 2000.

Weizmann was born on Nov. 27, 1874, in Motol, Russia, and he was educated in Germany and Switzerland. He taught chemistry at Manchester University in England from 1904 to 1914. During World War I, Weizmann discovered an improved method of making acetone and butyl alcohol for explosives. This discovery aided the United Kingdom's war effort.

On March 8, 1920, Palestinian Arabs demonstrated outside the Damascus Gate in Jerusalem against establishing a national homeland in Palestine for the Jewish people.

end to Jewish immigration and land purchase.

In 1939, the British began to set limits on Jewish immigration to Palestine. Palestine's Jews fought against the restrictions. They felt the restrictions kept many Jews from fleeing persecution in Europe.

During World War II (1939-1945), German Nazi dictator Adolf Hitler tried to kill all of Europe's Jews. Consequently, about 6 million Jews were murdered in what is called the *Holocaust* (*HOL uh kawst*). (Millions of others considered undesirable by the Nazis also were murdered, including persons with physical or mental handicaps, Roma [sometimes called Gypsies], Slavs, Soviet prisoners of war, homosexuals, Jehovah's

Israel's declaration of independence in 1948 led to the first Arab-Israeli war. Hours after Israeli leader David Ben-Gurion (above, standing) read the declaration, Arab forces invaded Israel.

Witnesses, priests and ministers, labor unionists, Communists, and other political opponents.) After World War II ended, the Zionists wanted to establish a Jewish state immediately to provide a homeland for Holocaust survivors. Most of the countries that defeated Germany supported the idea of creating a new Jewish state where Jews would be safe from persecution. But Arabs continued to oppose the creation of a Jewish state in Palestine. In 1947, the United Kingdom submitted the problem to the United Nations.

On Nov. 29, 1947, the United Nations approved a plan to divide Palestine into two states, one Jewish and the other Palestinian. Zionist leaders accepted the plan. But Arab governments and the Palestinians saw the division as the theft of Arab land by Zionists and the governments that supported them. Fighting broke out immediately.

British rule over Palestine ended when Zionists proclaimed the state of Israel on May 14, 1948. That day, the nation of Israel officially came into being.

David Ben-Gurion (*behn GOO rih uhn*) (1886-1973) served as the first prime minister of Israel after it became independent. He served two terms, the first from 1949 to 1953 and another from 1955 to 1963. He had previously been chairman of the Executive of the Jewish Agency for Palestine from 1935 to 1948. Ben-Gurion directed all Jewish affairs in the country with activities ranging from land development and settlement of immigrants to secret activities against Arabs and the British.

Ben-Gurion was born David Green in Plonsk, Russia (now in Poland), on Oct. 16, 1886. He settled in Palestine in 1906. By 1919, he was a Zionist leader, working to create a Jewish state in Palestine. In 1930, he founded the Mapai (*muh PY*) (Israel Workers' Party). He was a secretary-general of the Histadrut (*hihs tuh DROOT*) (General Federation of Labor) from 1921 to 1935.

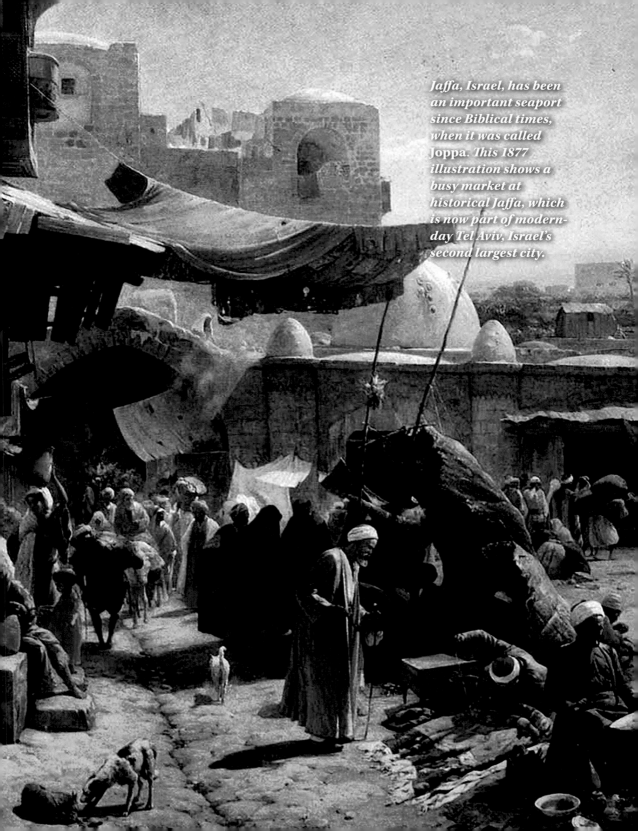

Jaffa, Israel, has been an important seaport since Biblical times, when it was called Joppa. This 1877 illustration shows a busy market at historical Jaffa, which is now part of modern-day Tel Aviv, Israel's second largest city.

CHAPTER TWO

Arabs, their land and their history

Arabs are a large group of people whose native language is Arabic. Arabs also share a common history and culture. Most Arabs live in the Middle East, a large region that spreads across southwestern Asia and northern Africa. Arabs have also migrated to other countries. European countries with large Arab populations include Belgium, France, Germany, the Netherlands, Sweden, and the United Kingdom. In South America, Argentina and Brazil have many Arab people. Canada and the United States in North America also have significant Arab populations.

There are two chief definitions of the Arab world. One is a political definition. The other is a *linguistic* (language-related) one. Politically, the Arab world is usually said to include 18 states. In Asia, these states are Iraq, Jordan, Kuwait, Lebanon, Oman, Qatar, Saudi Arabia, Syria, the United Arab Emirates, and Yemen. The Arab states in Africa are Algeria, Bahrain, Egypt, Libya, Mauritania, Morocco, Sudan, and Tunisia. All 18 states are called Arab states because most of their people are Arabs and their governments regard themselves as Arab. Three other countries—Djibouti, Somalia, and Comoros—have only small Arab populations. But they are sometimes included in this political definition because they belong to an organization of Arab states called the Arab League.

The Palestine Liberation Organization is also a member of the Arab League. The PLO represents Arabs working to establish an Arab state in the West Bank and Gaza areas of Palestine. The organization is approved by Arab countries to represent the Palestinians.

In a linguistic sense, the term *Arab world* refers to those areas where most people speak Arabic as their native language. This linguistic definition differs from the political one because some Arab countries include large areas populated by non-Arabs. Some non-Arab countries also have significant Arab minorities. For example, the Kurds of Iraq and the Berbers of northern Africa are non-Arabs living in Arab countries. At the same time, many Arabs live within the borders of such non-Arab nations as Iran and Israel. In this book, the term *Arab world* chiefly refers to the countries usually considered Arab in a political sense.

The word *Arab* was probably originally associated with tribes of the Arabian Peninsula and nearby Middle East. These tribes lived a nomadic lifestyle of herding camels. By about 400 B.C., the word was also applied to the settled people in these areas who spoke the Arabic language. The number of Arabs who follow a nomadic way of life gradually shrank over the centuries. By A.D. 850, many settled people in the region identified themselves as Arabs. Arabic had become the standard language of trade and religious discussions by this time. Today, almost all Arabs live in cities, towns, and villages.

Arabs today are united mainly by their culture. Among the most important aspects of Arab culture are the Arabic language and shared social values. The Arabs also have common traditions in literature, art, and music. Religious and historical factors also bind the Arabs together. Most Arabs are Muslims, followers of a religion called Islam. The Arabs' rise to political and cultural importance during the A.D. 600's and 700's was closely associated with the rise of Islam.

Another bond among all Arabs is their shared pride in classical Arab and Islamic civilization. The modern Arab identity emerged during the

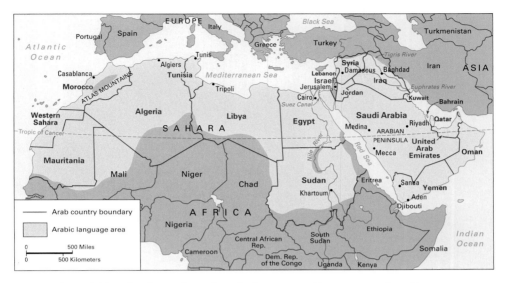

The Arab world has both a political and a linguistic (language-related) definition. Politically, it includes 18 countries (shown here) in the Middle East and across northern Africa. Western Sahara (also shown) is claimed by Morocco. In a linguistic sense, the Arab world refers to the areas where most people speak Arabic as their native language.

1800's and 1900's. During that period, most Arab lands were colonies of European powers. So, Arabs also share a sense of themselves as former subjects of European rule.

Despite this common heritage, deep differences exist among the Arab countries. For example, many Arab countries possess valuable petroleum deposits. The export of oil has made some countries, such as Kuwait and Qatar, rich. But such countries as Sudan and Yemen remain poor. Some countries, including Jordan and Lebanon, have highly urban societies. Many people in those countries work in industry or commerce. Others, such as Mauritania and Yemen, have largely rural societies. There, many people are farmers or herders. Some countries, such as Lebanon and Tunisia, have been heavily influenced by European and

Arabs, their land and their history   25

American culture. Others, such as Saudi Arabia, have chosen to maintain traditional culture in many areas of life. These and other differences have caused conflicts, and even wars, within the Arab world.

The Arab world extends over about 5 million square miles (13 million square kilometers), covering roughly three main regions. These regions are the Arabian Peninsula (sometimes called Arabia); northern Africa; and part of an area called the Fertile Crescent. The Fertile Crescent includes Iraq, Jordan, Lebanon, Syria, and historical Palestine. Today,

Palestine consists of the non-Arab state of Israel and the Arab areas of the Gaza Strip and the West Bank.

Despite the vast area of the Arab world, only a small percentage of it is suitable for settlement. Much of the region is extremely hot and dry. It has large deserts. These barren regions include the Sahara of northern Africa, the deserts of the Arabian Peninsula, and the Syrian Desert. At the other extreme are snow-capped mountains. They include Mount Lebanon in Lebanon and the peaks of the High Atlas range in Morocco.

Almost all Arabs live in well-watered hilly regions, fertile river valleys, and humid coastal areas. The most densely settled area is the Nile Valley and Nile River Delta of Egypt. Virtually all the people of Egypt—almost a third of all Arabs—live in this area. Many of Iraq's people live in the fertile area between the Tigris (*TY grihs*) and Euphrates (*yoo FRAY teez*) rivers. The Valley of the Orontes (*awr ON teez*) River in Syria is likewise densely populated. Other population centers include the coastal and hill zones of northwestern Africa and of Lebanon, Syria, and parts of Palestine.

Historically, a scarcity of water hampered population growth and economic development in the dry areas of the Middle East. Irrigation has expanded the amount of land that can be farmed in many regions. However, sizable Arab cities have long existed even in dry areas. Cities of the Arab world thrived in the desert mainly because they lay at the cross-roads of major trade routes.

About half of all Arabs live in cities and large towns. Many of these people work in factories or in such fields as business, government, and health care. Most other Arabs live in villages or small towns. They work as farmers or in local trades. In many Arab countries, the creation of modern road networks has enabled industries to spread to rural areas. As a result, some villagers have jobs in nearby factories. In the oil-producing countries of the Arab world, a large percentage of the male population works in the petroleum industry.

In the past, many Arabs were nomadic herders. They lived in tents and crossed the desert with their camels, sheep, goats, or cattle in search of water and grazing land. Today, few Arabs are nomads. Livestock herding now resembles ranching rather than nomadic life. Herders usually transport their animals—even camels—by truck.

Arabic belongs to the Semitic group of languages. This group also includes Hebrew and Aramaic (*ar uh MAY ihk*). Virtually all people who consider themselves Arab speak Arabic as their native language. But different forms of spoken Arabic, called *dialects,* vary considerably from one region to another. A common form of Arabic taught in schools is used to communicate across different dialects. This type of Arabic is called Modern Standard Arabic (MSA) in English or *Fus-ha* in Arabic. MSA is a modernized and simplified version of classical Arabic. MSA serves as the chief form of written Arabic. It is also the language used in mosques and universities. People speak it in public speeches and at other formal events. Radio and television broadcast in MSA throughout the Arab world. Most Arabs know and use two different forms of Arabic. They use their own native dialect in informal settings. They speak MSA for formal occasions and also use it in written communication. Arabs today are increasingly familiar with MSA because of a rise in literacy and exposure to television and other media.

Many other languages are used in various parts of the Arab world. For example, many people speak French in the former French colonies of Algeria, Morocco, and Tunisia. Many Arabs also learn English.

More than 90 percent of Arabs are Muslims. Most belong to the Sunni (*SOON ee* or *SUN nee*) branch of Islam. However, significant Shī`ite (*SHEE eyet*) Muslim communities exist in Iraq, the eastern Arabian Peninsula, Bahrain, and Lebanon. Some Shī`ites live in most other Arab countries. Small numbers of Arabs belong to other Muslim groups. Druses (*DROOZ ehz*), who follow a religion related to Islam, live mainly in Lebanon, Syria, and Palestine.

Most non-Muslim Arabs are Christians. The Copts of Egypt belong to one of the oldest Christian groups. Other Christian Arabs belong to various Eastern Orthodox, Roman Catholic, or Protestant churches. They live mainly in Iraq, Jordan, Lebanon, Syria, and Palestine. Most of the

Christians in Palestine and adjoining areas are the descendants of the oldest Christian communities in the world.

References to Arabs as nomads and camel herders of northern Arabia appear in writings dating back to the 800's B.C. The name *Arab* was later applied to all inhabitants of the Arabian Peninsula, and others in Syria and Iraq who spoke Arabic. Arabs at that time were a tribal society. Groups were organized by family lineages (*LIHN ee ihj uhz* – a lineage is a descent in a direct line from an ancestor) that all traced their origins back to a common ancestor. Politically, tribal society in the Arabian Peninsula was fragmented. Tribes typically broke up into smaller clans that roamed the desert, occasionally stopping at oases and wells for food and water.

About the 400's B.C., some Arab families established several small states in the Arabian Peninsula at centers for the overland caravan trade. One of these states centered in Petra, in what is now Jordan. Arabs known as Nabataeans founded Petra. The Roman Empire conquered Petra in A.D. 106, but it continued to flourish until the early A.D. 200's. Another state centered around the oasis of Palmyra in the Syrian Desert. Palmyra also fell under Roman domination by about A.D. 160.

The prophet Muhammad (*moo HAM uhd*), one of history's most important figures, was born in the Arab city of Mecca about A.D. 570. Muslims believe that God revealed the teachings of Islam to Muhammad, who began preaching about 610. *Islam* is an Arabic word that means *surrender* or *submission*. Today, Islam is the world's second largest religion, after Christianity.

Muhammad preached a *monotheistic* (*mon uh thee IHS tihk*) *religion* (belief in one God), like that of Jews and Christians. He fled with his followers north to Medina (*muh DEE nuh*), then called Yathrib (*YATH rihb*) in 622 when pagan Arabs of Mecca opposed him. This year became

Muslim pilgrims pray at the Kaaba (above), the holiest shrine of Islam.
The Kaaba is an empty cube-shaped building that stands in the center of
the Great Mosque in the city of Mecca, Saudi Arabia. All adult Muslims
must make at least one pilgrimage to Mecca during their lifetime.

known as the year of the Hijrah (migration), also spelled *Hijra* or *Hegira*.
It later became the first year of the Islamic calendar. In Medina, Muhammad organized his followers into a community. This community quickly
grew into a state that controlled much of the Arabian Peninsula. Today,
Mecca and Medina are Islam's two holiest cities.

After Muhammad's death in 632, Muslim rulers called *caliphs* (*KAY lihf*

During the 1600's, the Ottoman Empire was the world's largest empire. It had its capital in Constantinople (today's city of Istanbul) in what is now Turkey and covered parts of Eastern Europe, the Middle East, and North Africa.

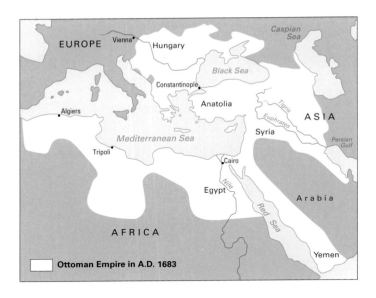

or *KAL ihf*) headed the Islamic state. Armies under the caliphs soon seized the rest of Arabia and an area stretching from Egypt to Iran. The result was a vast and expanding new empire dominated by Arabian Muslims. Islam was the official religion of the empire. Arabic was its official language.

For several hundred years, the political life of the empire was dominated by three families from Muhammad's tribe of Quraysh (*kawr ysh*). These families were the Umayyads (*oo MY adhz*), the Abbasids (*uh BAS ihdz* or *AB uh sihdz*), and the Alids (*AL ihdz*). The Umayyads ruled from 661 to 750. Their capital was Damascus (*duh MAS kuhs*). They extended the empire as far west as Spain and as far east as India. In 750, the Umayyads were overthrown by the Abbasids, though the Umayyads retained control of Spain. The Abbasids built themselves a splendid new capital in Iraq, called Baghdad. After about 850, the Abbasids increasingly lost control of distant parts of the empire. The distant areas became independent under local Islamic *dynasties* (ruling families). The

Alids, the main rivals of the Umayyads and Abbasids, made many unsuccessful attempts to overthrow them. The Alids finally established the Fātimid (*FAT uh mihd*) dynasty in northern Africa in 909. For their capital in Egypt, the Fātimids founded the city of Cairo. They ruled over Egypt until 1171.

A sense of Arab identity seems to have emerged in connection with the spread of Islam. This sense of "Arabness" resulted partly from use of the Arabic language and partly from pride in the Islamic Empire. It also stemmed from identification with the rich literary and scientific culture that developed under the Umayyads and Abbasids.

From the 1000's to the 1500's, parts of the eastern Arab lands were conquered by several waves of non-Arab invaders. Chief among these were the Seljuk (*sehl JOOK*) Turks and the Mongols. The Mongols executed the last Abbasid caliph in Baghdad in 1258. Northern Africa remained in the hands of local groups, mainly Arabs and Berbers.

By the mid-1500's, nearly all Arab territories had come under the control of the Ottoman Empire. It centered in what is now the nation of Turkey and stretched far into Europe. The Arab lands were an important part of the empire. Many high-ranking Ottoman officials were of Arab origin. But these Arabs regarded themselves as Ottomans and Muslims, not as Arabs.

Beginning in the mid-1700's, the rapid economic and military development of much of Europe gave European states an advantage over the Ottomans. In their efforts to modernize their economies, the Ottomans often developed large debts to European financiers. The financiers then sometimes persuaded their governments to seize economic or political control of Ottoman possessions to ensure payment of the debts. In other cases, European nations simply invaded Ottoman territories. France began its occupation of Algeria in 1830. It controlled Tunisia and

Morocco by the early 1900's. Beginning in the late 1800's, the United Kingdom took over Egypt and Sudan. Italy gained control of Libya in 1912. By the start of World War I in 1914, all of northern Africa was under European control. The United Kingdom also controlled many of the affairs of the small Arab states surrounding the Persian Gulf.

The Ottoman Empire entered World War I on the side of Germany. Then, the United Kingdom helped stir up an Arab nationalist revolt against the Ottomans. The United Kingdom promised the leaders of the revolt that it would recognize an independent Arab government in former Ottoman territories after the war. But the United Kingdom also made a secret agreement with France to divide these territories into British and French spheres of influence after the war.

When World War I ended in 1918, the League of Nations—a forerunner of today's United Nations—divided the Arab areas still held by the Ottomans between the United Kingdom and France. In turn, the United Kingdom and France were expected to supervise these lands and help them attain self-government. The supervised lands were known as *mandated territories*—colonies and territories taken from defeated nations and placed under the administration of one or more of the victorious nations. The United Kingdom received mandates over Iraq and Palestine, which included present-day Jordan and Israel. France received what are now Syria and Lebanon.

Arab nationalism arose as the nationalist idea spread through much of the world during the 1800's and 1900's. This idea centered on the belief that humanity was divided into distinct nations or peoples. The members of each nation shared a common history and language. Each nation had a historic claim to a particular homeland.

Among most Arabs, Islam remained the main binding force for many years. Significant Arab nationalist movements did not develop until the

In December 1917, British troops captured the city of Jerusalem and ended Ottoman control over the city. The mayor of Jerusalem, Hussein al-Husseini (above, with cane), meets with the British under the white flag of surrender.

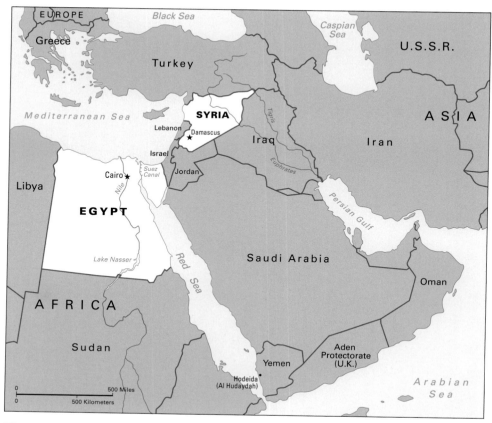

The United Arab Republic (U.A.R.) was a union of two
independent Middle Eastern countries, Egypt and Syria.
President Gamal Abdel Nasser of Egypt and Shukri
al-Kuwatly of Syria formed the union on Feb. 1, 1958.
Syrian rebels ended it on Sept. 29, 1961, setting up an
independent government for Syria.

early 1900's. The movements took two forms. In some cases, nationalist
feelings arose around particular areas or regions as a form of patriotism.
In others, it centered on factors of common descent and the shared
Arabic language as sources of unity, later growing into a movement for
Arab political unification called *Pan-Arabism*.

By the early 1920's, the main population centers in the Arab world had been split into more than 15 European colonies and *protectorates* (territories under partial control). The influence of the colonial powers divided these colonies politically, economically, and culturally. Because of these divisions, the goal of Pan-Arab unification became less important than that of independence within each colony.

Most of the Arab lands won their independence in stages after World War II (1939-1945) ended. Some did so peacefully. Others had to struggle. The last colonies to become independent—British-controlled Bahrain, Qatar, and the states that now make up the United Arab Emirates—did so in 1971.

Arab countries emerged from colonial rule as free and independent states. But most continue to struggle with many problems. Modern Arab countries face significant challenges. These challenges include a lack of unity in the Arab world and economic inequality between and within Arab states. Sources of friction include the Arab-Israeli conflict and religious and ethnic conflicts.

Many Arab states also lack democratically elected governments. The Arab world has a significant role in world affairs due to its location and the petroleum reserves that it owns. As a result, foreign interest and foreign involvement in Arab politics represent another challenge that modern Arabs must face. Many conflicts in the Arab world arise between Islamic tradition and the influence of the West—that is, Europe and the United States.

The search for unity among all Arab countries has not been successful. Several times, two or three Arab countries have attempted to unite into a single state. For example, Syria and Egypt joined to form the United Arab Republic in 1958, but the union ended when Syria withdrew in 1961. In 1945, seven countries founded the Arab League. Today, 21 countries and the region of Palestine belong to the league.

Arab League

The Arab League is an organization of 22 Middle Eastern and African countries where Arabic is the main spoken language. Its official name is the League of Arab States. The league regards Palestine, represented by the Palestinian Authority, as a country. The Pact of the League of Arab States sets out that the organization promotes improved political, economic, cultural, and social relations among its members.

A council of representatives from the member states works to settle disputes peacefully. It can also decide how to repel aggression against a member. League activities are carried out by a number of committees, including those on economic, legal, Palestinian, political, and social and cultural affairs.

The league's charter was signed in 1945 by seven countries—Egypt, Iraq, Lebanon, Saudi Arabia, Syria, Transjordan (now Jordan), and Yemen (Sanaa). Since then, 16 other members have joined—Libya (1953), Sudan (1956), Morocco (1958), Tunisia (1958), Kuwait (1961), Algeria (1962), Yemen (Aden, 1967), Bahrain (1971), Oman (1971), Qatar (1971), United Arab Emirates (1971), Mauritania (1973), Somalia (1974), Palestine (1976), Djibouti (1977), and Comoros (1993). In 1990, Yemen (Aden) and Yemen (Sanaa) united as Yemen.

The Arab League has had difficulty living up to the aspirations of its founders. Political differences, suspicions, and rivalries have made the league's political and defense agreements largely ineffective. However, the league has achieved some success in expressing the rights of Palestinians. In 1974, it helped Palestinians attain observer status at the United Nations. Observers have the right to speak at UN meetings but not to vote on resolutions.

The Arab League's greatest accomplishments have probably been those in the social, cultural, and communications fields. The formation in 1976 of ARABSAT, an Arab communications satellite system, helped foster cooperation among Arab countries. The league has also worked to preserve Arabic language and heritage and to modernize school courses.

The Arab League has often reflected rather than settled disputes among its members. In 1979, Egypt signed a peace treaty with Israel. Because Arab countries at that time had no diplomatic relations with Israel, the league suspended Egypt's membership. It also transferred its headquarters from Cairo, Egypt, to Tunis, Tunisia. The league readmitted Egypt in 1989 and returned its headquarters to Cairo in 1990. In 1994, Jordan signed a treaty with Israel, but was not punished by the league.

After Iraq invaded Kuwait in 1990, most league members approved of the use of military force to expel Iraq from Kuwait. But in 2003, only Kuwait supported a United States-led war against Iraq. Some other members, including Bahrain and Qatar, allowed their territory to be used for planning and staging the war effort.

In 2002, the Arab League approved a peace plan, sponsored by Saudi Arabia, between its members and Israel. However, Israel did not agree with many of the plan's terms. In 2005 and 2007, the league revived the plan, but Israel has not yet accepted it.

Oil wells burned out of control in Kuwait after retreating Iraqi troops set fire to hundreds of wells during the Persian Gulf War of 1991. The dense smoke from the fires darkened the skies in Kuwait and caused serious air pollution in the country, as well as in Iran, Iraq, and other parts of Asia.

The Arab-Israeli conflict can best be understood as a struggle between two nationalist movements. Both movements claim Palestine as their homeland. During World War I, British officials had suggested to Arab leaders that Palestine would be included in areas to be granted Arab self-determination. However, the British also promised Palestine to leaders of the Zionist movement. The Zionists sought to make Palestine an independent Jewish nation. The conflicting promises to Arabs and Zionists regarding Palestine contributed to a struggle between the two nationalist movements.

More than 700,000 Arabs were forced to flee Palestine following the creation of the Jewish state of Israel in 1948. This set off hostilities that led to five wars between Israel and Arab countries from 1948 to 1982. The conflict continues today.

The different economic needs and political goals of Arab states have, at times, made them bitter rivals. The wealth of some Arab countries from petroleum exports has contributed to tension. Petroleum-poor states resent the wealth of their richer neighbors and seek to share in the oil income. Disagreements have also occurred among petroleum exporters over pricing and production policies.

Disagreements regarding petroleum wealth helped set off an invasion of Kuwait by Iraq in 1990. Iraq's president, Saddam Hussein (*sah DAHM hoo SAYN*) (1937-2006), wished to gain control of Kuwait's vast oil reserves. The subsequent war severely divided Arab states. Several Arab countries, including Saudi Arabia and Egypt, took part in a coalition led by the United States that fought the Persian Gulf War of 1991 and expelled Iraqi forces from Kuwait.

Territorial ambitions or religious differences between Arab countries or between groups within the countries themselves have led to other clashes in the Arab world. For example, a long and bloody conflict in Lebanon began in 1975. It reflected the struggle for political power between Christian and Muslim religious communities. Both Christian and Muslim sects also began fighting among themselves. The civil war did not end until 1991.

In Iraq, old ethnic hostilities between Iraqi Arabs and Kurds emerged after the Persian Gulf War of 1991 and the Iraq War (2003-2011). The Kurds are Iraq's largest non-Arab ethnic minority. Old religious tensions between Iraqi Sunni and Shi`ite Muslims also erupted following the war.

A small number of powerful people dominate political life in most Arab

In late 2010 and 2011, antigovernment protests erupted in several Arab countries. The unrest was fueled in part by poor economic conditions and accusations of government corruption. On Feb. 1, 2011, tens of thousands of Egyptians gathered in Tahrir Square (right) in Cairo, Egypt, in a massive antigovernment demonstration. The protests in Cairo and other cities across Egypt forced longtime President Hosni Mubarak from power days later.

lands. The ruling group may consist of military leaders or wealthy individuals of prominent tribal background. The European powers took some limited steps toward developing institutions of democratic government in their Arab colonies. But they kept such institutions from becoming strong enough to threaten their colonial rule. They also failed to create economic or educational systems that would stimulate the growth of a middle class. As a result, most independent Arab states lack strong institutions of multiparty, civilian government.

The United States led a coalition of nations in a war that toppled the Iraqi regime of Saddam Hussein in 2003. Coalition troops invaded the country from Kuwait in the south. However, most other Arab countries opposed this war. Many Arabs saw the war as an intervention by the United States in Arab affairs. The war contributed to widespread feel-

ings of anti-Americanism among citizens of Arab countries and other, non-Arab Islamic states. Many nationalist Arabs blame their current lack of political rights on the long periods of oppressive European colonialism. They also blame the United States for its support of Saudi Arabia and other undemocratic regimes, and for its support of Israel.

In late 2010 and 2011, antigovernment protests erupted in several Arab countries. The protests were fueled in part by poor economic conditions and accusations of government corruption. Protesters clashed with government security forces in Bahrain, Egypt, Libya, Syria, Tunisia, and Yemen. The presidents of Tunisia, Egypt, and Yemen stepped down. In Libya, the protests led to an armed rebellion that overthrew Mu'ammar Muhammad al-Qadhafi (*moo ahm MAHR moo HAM uhd ahl guhd DAH fee*) (1942-2011).

U.S. Census Bureau figures show that about 1.75 million Arab Americans live in the United States. On July 3, 1986, Hassan Mahmoud (shown here) sang patriotic songs to his son during the largest citizenship ceremony ever in the United States. He was among 14,200 immigrants from 67 countries who took the oath of citizenship in Miami, Florida.

CHAPTER THREE

Arabs and Arabic culture in America

Arab Americans are Americans who have roots in the *Arab world*—that is, the areas where people speak the Arabic language and share other cultural traditions. The Arab world includes much of the Middle East, the region that spreads across southwestern Asia and northern Africa. The Arab world includes the historic region of Palestine. Palestine today consists of the state of Israel and two Palestinian territories, the West Bank and the Gaza Strip.

According to the U.S. Census Bureau, about 1.75 million Arab Americans live in the United States. About half of them have roots in either Egypt, Lebanon, or Syria. Large numbers also come from Iraq, Jordan, Morocco, and Palestine.

In the Middle East, more than 95 percent of Arabs are Muslims—that is, followers of the religion of Islam. However, less than half of all Arab Americans practice Islam. Many Arab Americans belong to Eastern Rite Churches, such as the Antiochian (*AN tee OH kee uhn*) Orthodox Church, the Coptic Church, and the Maronite Church. Eastern Rite Churches are independent but related Christian churches with roots in eastern Europe, Africa, and Asia. Other Arab American Christians belong to Roman Catholic and Protestant churches.

Many Arab Americans speak the Arabic language and emphasize the teaching of Arabic to children. Arab American Muslims especially stress the importance of Arabic, since it is the language of the Qur'an, the sacred book of Islam, and the language in which Muslims pray.

Arab Americans typically hold the same values that other Americans hold. They emphasize education, family, faith, and hospitality. In most cases, the lifestyles of Arab Americans are not different from other Americans. Some Arab American immigrants keep certain customs, habits, and traditions from their homelands. For example, an Arab American girl from a Muslim family might cover her hair with a head-scarf and still wear jeans and sneakers like other American girls.

Arab Americans live in all 50 states. The states with the largest Arab American populations are California, Michigan, and New York.

About 90 percent of Arab Americans live in urban areas. For many years, New York City was the main center for Arab immigrants in the United States. But during the late 1900's, the Detroit area emerged as the major hub of Arab American life and culture. Numerous Arab American cultural, business, and human service organizations are based in Detroit. Other major centers of Arab American life include Chicago; Los Angeles and other parts of southern California; Washington, D.C.; and parts of northeastern New Jersey.

Arab American accomplishments, as well as the traditions of the Arab world, have strongly influenced life and culture in the United States. Americans of Arab descent have made significant contributions to virtually every field and profession.

Michael E. DeBakey (1908-2008), a surgeon of Lebanese descent, won fame for his groundbreaking work with the heart and blood vessels. He also worked on the development of an artificial heart. Arab American scientists Elias J. Corey (1928-   ) and Ahmed H. Zewail (*zuh WAYL*) (1946-2016) won the Nobel Prize in chemistry in 1990 and 1999, respectively. Steve Jobs (1955-2011), the son of a Syrian immigrant father, cofounded the computer company Apple Inc. in 1976.

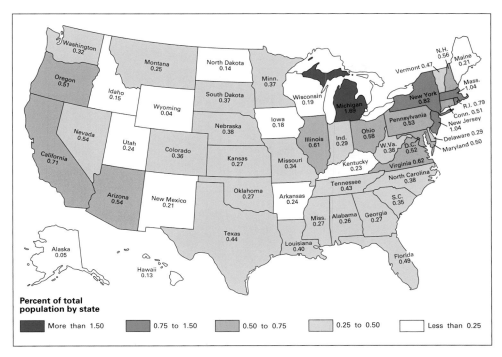

This map shows the state-by-state distribution of the Arab American population according to the 2010 census. The numbers on the map indicate the percentage of Arab Americans in the total population of each state.

George A. Kasem (1919-2002) was the first Arab American to serve in the U.S. Congress. Kasem, who represented California in the House of Representatives, was elected in 1958. Donna E. Shalala (1941-   ) was the first Arab American to serve in a U.S. president's Cabinet. She served as secretary of health and human services from 1993 to 2001. Ralph Nader (NAY duhr) (1934-   ), the son of Lebanese immigrants, is well known as a consumer advocate and presidential candidate.

Well-known Arab American entertainers have included the comedian and philanthropist Danny Thomas (1912-1991); the Emmy-winning actor Tony Shalhoub (1953-   ); and "American Top 40" disk jockey Casey

Kasem (1932-2014). Notable Arab American athletes have included football players John Elway (1960-) and Doug Flutie (1962-) and race car driver Bobby Rahal (1953-), as well as the Moroccan-born marathon runner Khalid Khannouchi (*KAH leed kah NOO chee*) (1971-).

Traditional aspects of Arab culture have become part of the daily life of many Americans. For instance, "pita" (*PEE tah*) bread and chickpea dishes—such as *hummus* (*HUHM uhs*) and *falafel* (*fuh LAH fuhl*)—are familiar foods for many people in the United States. In addition, some people use *couscous* (*KUS kus*), which is steamed cracked wheat, instead of rice in many dishes. Couscous originated in northern Africa.

During the mid-1900's, Arab Americans increasingly identified themselves as Americans, though they continued to establish mosques, Arab cultural organizations, charity groups, and Eastern Rite Churches in the United States. The Islamic Center of America (above) is a mosque in Dearborn, Michigan.

Henna (*HEHN uh*), a reddish dye, and *kohl*, a powder worn around the eyes, are common cosmetic products that have roots in the Arab world. *Raqs sharqi* (*rawks SHAHR kee*)—commonly known as *belly dancing*—is a Middle Eastern dance style that many people in the United States use as a form of exercise or entertainment. Many Americans also listen to Arab popular music or to regional styles, such as rai (*ry*) music. Rai music originated in Algeria and combines Arabic love poetry and Bedouin folk music. Modern rai has also been influenced by such genres as rock, flamenco, soul, and reggae.

Arab immigrants began settling in the United States in the 1880's. The first immigrants were mainly Christian Arabs from the lands that are now Lebanon and Syria, then part of the Ottoman Empire. They came to the United States in search of economic opportunity and freedom from famine and other harsh conditions. Most early Arab immigrants settled in commercial and industrial areas. By 1925, an estimated 200,000 Arabs were living in the United States.

During the late 1800's and early 1900's, many Arab immigrants faced challenges to their eligibility for U.S. citizenship. Many of these challenges involved special restrictions the U.S. government had placed on Asian immigration. Some judges denied Arab immigrants—most of whom came from southwestern Asia—the same rights granted to "white" immigrants at the time. Eventually, after many years of dispute, the Arab immigrants' eligibility for citizenship was confirmed.

Arab immigrants faced additional obstacles in the early 1900's, when *quotas* (limits) were placed on immigration from countries outside of northern Europe. Under the National Origins Act of 1924, the United States admitted only a few hundred Arab immigrants annually.

During the mid-1900's, a cultural transformation took place among many Arab Americans. They continued to organize around their Arab heritage—such as establishing Arab cultural organizations, charity groups, Eastern Rite Churches, and mosques—but they increasingly identified themselves as Americans. In the years surrounding World War II, Arab Americans were strongly patriotic, served in the military, and were proud of their U.S. citizenship. Most Arab American families focused heavily on education and economic advancement.

A new wave of Arab immigrants came to the United States after the government lifted nationality-based immigration quotas in the 1960's. Many immigrants came to avoid instability and violence associated with conflicts in newly independent Arab states. The Arab-Israeli wars of 1948 and 1967, for instance, displaced hundreds of thousands of Palestinians.

This second wave of immigrants came primarily from Egypt, Iraq, Jordan, Lebanon, Syria, and Palestine. The first wave of immigrants had been mainly Christians, but the new wave included large numbers of Muslims. Many of these Muslims faced unique challenges in balancing their religious lives with American culture. Many Americans knew little about—and sometimes were hostile to—Muslim beliefs and traditions.

The second wave of immigrants placed a heavy emphasis on ethnic identity and on the continuation of Arab traditions. Since the 1960's, numerous Arab American organizations have sought to assist Arab immigrants, foster ties with the Arab world, and promote use of the Arabic language. Some organizations specifically address the needs of Arab Americans of particular religious sects or countries of origin.

By the 1990's, more than 10,000 Arab immigrants arrived in the United States each year. In the late 1990's and early 2000's, changes in immigration law made it more difficult for Arabs to come to the United States.

The Arab American community has been directly affected by political instability in the Middle East; the terrorist attacks of Sept. 11, 2001; and

U.S. President George W. Bush (center) speaks with leaders of the Arab community after touring the Islamic Center in Washington, D.C. The meeting on Sept. 17, 2001, took place just days after Islamic extremists carried out the September 11 terrorists attacks against the United States.

hostilities between the United States and parts of the Arab world. Because the terrorists responsible for the September 11 attacks were Arab Muslims, some Americans began to treat Arab Americans with suspicion and hostility. Many innocent Arab Americans faced discrimination, harassment, threats, and violence in the months and years following the attacks. Many people argued that certain government actions unfairly targeted Arabs and Muslims in the United States. The Iraq War caused further difficulties for Arab Americans, especially those of Iraqi descent. The U.S. government and numerous Arab American organizations have worked to address these concerns and to eliminate discrimination.

Since 2001, the Arab American community has actively sought to promote cultural understanding between Arab Americans and their fellow citizens. In addition, many Arab Americans have assisted the U.S. government by providing expertise on Arab culture and politics, and by working to build friendly relations between the United States and the Arab world.

Activist Islamist movements in the Arab world have long perceived European and American influences on traditional Arab Islamic culture as a threat. Such movements have also expressed frustration with the lack of democracy and the economic inequality in the Arab world. They are also frustrated with the ongoing Arab-Israeli conflict. Islamist movement groups often blame foreign powers, especially the United States, as the source of many or most of the problems Arabs face today.

Activist Islamist movements seek political, social, and economic reform. The goal of many movement groups is to ensure that Arab governments represent and uphold Islamic morality and Islamic values of social and economic justice. The movements often work to provide social services, such as free health care, for the poor. However, some groups have engaged in armed attacks against their own governments and sometimes against foreigners. Americans and Europeans often refer to activist Islamist movements as *militant Islam* or *radical Islam.* Some government leaders and media have tended to label all Islamist movement groups as terrorist organizations. Others point out that only a small number of such groups use violence or terrorism to achieve their goals.

One terrorist network, known as *al-Qa`ida (KY ih duh),* supports the activities of Muslim extremists around the world. Al-Qa`ida is an Arabic term that means *the base.* Its founder and leader was Osama bin Laden (1957?-2011), a Saudi-born millionaire. Al-Qa`ida believes that governments of Muslim countries that fail to follow Islamic law should be overthrown. Al-Qa`ida also considers the United States to be a primary enemy of Islam.

In 2001, members of al-Qa`ida launched terrorist attacks that destroyed the World Trade Center in New York City and damaged the Pentagon Building near Washington, D.C. Other terrorist attacks attributed to al-Qa`ida have occurred since. Most leaders in the Arab world have denounced these crimes and promised cooperation in helping to bring the terrorists to justice. Many prominent Muslim clerics also issued *fatwas* (legal opinions) that these attacks violated Islamic law. Osama bin Laden was killed in a U.S. military raid in Pakistan in 2011.

Arabs today take great pride in their cultural heritage but face major challenges. The problems of poverty, overpopulation, poor health care, and inadequate educational facilities are severe in some Arab states. In addition, the oil-rich states must plan carefully for the day when oil reserves run dry. Many of these countries are working to develop other economic activities that can help maintain their growth in the post-petroleum age. Finally, Arabs also must deal with powerful conflicts between Islamic tradition and the challenges of modernity.

On March 10, 1949, Israeli General Avraham Adan hoisted this makeshift flag of the new nation of Israel at the Jordanian outpost of Um Rash-Rash on the Gulf of Aqaba (AH kuh buh). *The famous flag-raising at what is now known as Elat* (EE lat) *at the northern tip of the Red Sea followed the first Arab-Israeli War, also called Israel's War of Independence.*

CHAPTER FOUR

Conflicts and attacks (1948-1976)

O n May 15, 1948, the day after Israel officially became a nation-state, armies of Egypt, Syria, Lebanon, Transjordan (which became known as Jordan in 1949), and Iraq attacked Israel. Israel fought back. In the war, Israel absorbed much of the land the United Nations had set aside for the Palestinians. Egypt and Jordan occupied the rest of the area that was assigned to the Palestinians. Egypt held the Gaza Strip, the small area between Israel and the Mediterranean Sea. Jordan held the West Bank, the territory between Israel and the Jordan River. Israel controlled the western half of Jerusalem, and Jordan held the eastern half. Israel incorporated the gained territory into the new country, adding about 150,000 resentful Arabs to its population. By August 1949, Israel and all five Arab states had agreed to end the fighting. But formal peace treaties were not signed because the Arab countries refused to recognize the existence of Israel.

Because of the war, more than 700,000 Palestinians became refugees. Most fled to Jordan—including the West Bank—or to the Gaza Strip. Others went to Lebanon and Syria.

Border clashes between Arab and Israeli troops occurred frequently in the early 1950's. In the mid-1950's, Egypt began giving financial aid and military supplies to Palestinian Arab *fedayeen (fehd ah YEEN)*. The fedayeen (commandos) raided Israel from the Gaza Strip, the Egyptian-occupied part of Palestine. The Israelis raided the Gaza Strip in return.

In the 1950's, nationalism spread among the Arab countries of the

Gamal Abdel Nasser

Gamal Abdel Nasser *(gah MAHL AHB duhl NAH sehr)* (1918-1970) led the revolt that overthrew King Faruk (*fuh ROOK*) (1920-1965) in 1952 and made Egypt a republic. Nasser served as Egypt's prime minister from 1954 until he was elected president in 1956. Later in 1956, a world crisis occurred after Egypt *nationalized* (took control of) the Suez Canal, then under  British and French control. Nasser wanted to use the money generated by the canal to build the Aswan *(AS wahn* or *ahs WAHN)* High Dam. When Syria and Egypt formed the United Arab Republic (U.A.R.) in 1958, Nasser served as its president. Syria withdrew from the U.A.R. in 1961.

Nasser resigned after Egypt lost the Sinai *(SY ny)* Peninsula in the Arab-Israeli war of 1967. But the Egyptian people and the National Assembly refused to accept his resignation. He became both president and prime minister. Fighting between the Arab countries and Israel continued into the 1970's. In August 1970, Nasser agreed to a 90-day cease-fire with Israel. He died on Sept. 28, 1970.

Nasser's book *Egypt's Liberation: The Philosophy of the Revolution* (1955) stated his aims to unite all Arabs under Egyptian leadership and to liberate Egypt from colonialism and underdevelopment. He was unable to unite the Arab world, but he did become one of its most influential leaders. Nasser favored a neutral for-

Egyptian President Gamal Abdel Nasser (left) receives the Indian journalist R.K. Karanjia and his wife in 1958. Nasser came to power after leading a revolt that overthrew Egyptian King Faruk in 1952 and served as prime minister from 1954 until he was elected president in 1956. He later became both president and prime minister and remained in office until his sudden death on Sept. 28, 1970.

eign policy and emphasized nationalism and economic reform. He redistributed land to farmers and advanced education. However, his efforts to develop Egypt's economy were hampered by overpopulation and poverty.

Nasser was born on Jan. 15, 1918, in Alexandria, Egypt. He graduated from the Royal Military Academy in Cairo in 1938. He fought in the Arab war against Israel in 1948 and 1949.

Middle East. Egyptian President Gamal Abdel Nasser and his followers sought to rid Arab lands of the influence of Western nations.

During this time, Western countries, led by the United States, and Communist countries, led by the Soviet Union, both tried to gain influence in Egypt. The two *blocs* (groups of countries) were engaged in an intense rivalry known as the Cold War. Nasser wanted Egypt to remain neutral in the Cold War. He sought funding from both sides for economic development projects in Egypt.

In September 1955, Nasser signed an arms deal with Communist Czechoslovakia. (The one nation of Czechoslovakia was divided into the Czech Republic and Slovakia in 1993.) Under the agreement, Egypt received military equipment, including Soviet aircraft and tanks, in

The Suez Canal is a narrow, artificial waterway in Egypt that joins the Mediterranean and Red seas. The main canal is just under 100 miles (160 kilometers) long. Including entrance canals at both ends, the Suez Canal is about 120 miles (195 kilometers) long. A ship sailing between London, England, and Mumbai, India, saves about 5,100 miles (8,200 kilometers) by using the canal rather than traveling around Africa.

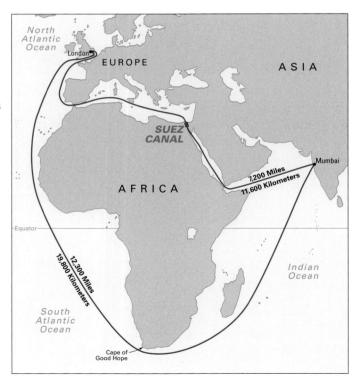

Egyptian President Gamal Abdel Nasser observes the construction of the Aswan High Dam on the Nile River in southeastern Egypt. Construction of the rock-filled dam began in 1960. The dam began operating in 1968.

exchange for cotton and rice. The United Kingdom and the United States opposed this deal. They were also troubled by Egypt's refusal to join an anti-Communist alliance and by its recognition of the Communist government in China.

In July 1956, the United States and the United Kingdom abruptly decided not to provide the funding they had earlier promised for construction of the Aswan High Dam. Nasser, angered by this action, quickly responded by *nationalizing* (taking control of) the Suez *(soo EHZ)* Canal Company, the international company that owned the Suez Canal. He planned to use revenue from the canal to pay for the dam. The canal continued to operate normally after the Egyptian takeover.

Pre-1950 history of the Suez Canal

The Suez Canal is a narrow, artificial waterway in Egypt that joins the Mediterranean Sea and the Red Sea. Including its entrance canals, the Suez Canal extends about 120 miles (195 kilometers). The main canal is almost 100 miles (160 kilometers) long. When it opened in 1869, the Suez Canal reduced the shipping route between London in the United Kingdom and Mumbai, India, by nearly half. The canal is one of the busiest *interoceanic* (between oceans) waterways in the world.

The Suez Canal stretches north and south across the Isthmus of Suez, between the cities of Port Said *(sah EED)* and Suez. It has no *canal locks* (chambers that enable ships to move from one water level to another) because there is no great difference between the levels of the Red and Mediterranean seas. Most of the canal can handle only single-direction traffic. When the canal was built, it measured 26 feet (8 meters) deep, 72 feet (22 meters) wide at the bottom, and about 230 feet (70 meters) wide at the surface. It has since been enlarged several times. In the early 2010's, its minimum depth was 66 feet (20 meters) and its narrowest section was 741 feet (226 meters) wide at the surface.

In 1854, the French diplomat and engineer Ferdinand de Lesseps—a friend of Said Pasha *(sah EED PAH shuh)*, Egypt's ruler— obtained permission to build the Suez Canal. By 1858, the Suez Canal Company had been organized with a capital stock of about $40 million. However, the terms of the agreement were unfavorable toward Egypt. Construction on the canal, with Egyptian workers and equipment, began on April 25, 1859. Many Egyptian workers lost their lives during construction. The canal officially opened on

The Suez Canal, in Egypt, links the Mediterranean Sea and the Red Sea. The above illustration shows the first ships using the canal at its official opening in 1869.

Nov. 17, 1869. The Suez Canal Company was given a concession to operate the canal until 1968.

The unfavorable terms of the agreement, combined with Egypt's large debt, forced the country to sell its shares in the canal in 1875. The United Kingdom purchased the shares. After that, a commission composed mostly of British and French members directed the management of the canal. The United Kingdom occupied Egypt in 1882, mostly to protect its investment in the canal.

In 1888, an international convention agreed that the canal should be open to all nations in peace and in war. However, the United Kingdom kept nations at war with it from using the canal during World War I (1914-1918) and World War II (1939-1945). In 1922, Egypt gained independence from the United Kingdom, though the British kept many powers. A 1936 treaty restricted British troops to the canal zone.

Nasser took control of the Suez Canal from its British and French owners on July 26, 1956. The canal is a key shipping route between Europe and Asia.

Many countries protested Nasser's action. The United Kingdom, France, and Israel secretly plotted to end Egypt's control of the canal. The United Kingdom and France, which held controlling interest in the Suez Canal Company, began concentrating troops in the eastern Mediterranean area. At the time, Israel was also preparing for conflict with Egypt. Israeli and Egyptian troops had been engaging in raids and counterraids in the Gaza Strip, the Egyptian-administered part of Palestine. France, the United Kingdom, and Israel joined together in a secret plan to overthrow Nasser and regain control of the Suez Canal.

On October 29, Israel attacked and quickly defeated Egyptian forces in Egypt's Sinai Peninsula, an area of about 23,400 square miles (60,700 square kilometers) in southwestern Asia and holding about 500,000 people, between Israel and the canal.

The western part of Egypt and the Sinai Peninsula were first linked together as a province of the Islamic Empire in the A.D. 600's. In 1906, an agreement between the United Kingdom and the Ottoman Empire gave Egypt control over the peninsula.

The United Kingdom and France demanded that both Israel and Egypt withdraw from the canal zone and allow a joint British-French force to occupy the area. Israel, with British and French help, occupied most of the peninsula. On October 31, the United Kingdom and France began airstrikes against Egypt. In early November, French and British troops captured Port Said and Port Fuad (*foo AHD)*, two large ports in the canal zone. Thousands of Egyptian civilians and soldiers were killed or wounded in the fighting.

The United States, the Soviet Union, and many other countries con-

This map shows the location of the Suez Canal, a narrow, artificial waterway in Egypt. The canal joins the Mediterranean and Red seas. It stretches north and south across the Isthmus of Suez, between the cities of Port Said and Suez.

Port Said
Lake Manzilah
Mediterranean Sea
To Gaza
North
SUEZ CANAL
Al Ballah bypass
Sinai Peninsula
Ismailia
Lake Timsah
Expansion
E G Y P T
Great Bitter Lake
Faid
Expansion
Little Bitter Lake
SUEZ CANAL
To Cairo
Suez
Road
Railroad
0   10 Miles
0   10 Kilometers
Gulf of Suez

demned the invasion. The Soviet Union threatened armed intervention, and the United States warned of the possibility of a nuclear confrontation between the Soviet and Western blocs.

The United Nations called a ceasefire on November 6. A UN peacekeeping force was sent to Egypt. The UN force finished evacuating the French and British troops in December.

The United Kingdom and France were compensated for the shares they had held in the Suez Canal. But the two countries lost influence in the Middle East. Anthony Eden, the British prime minister, received harsh criticism for his handling of the Suez crisis. On Jan. 9, 1957, he resigned.

By March, Israel, under international pressure, returned the Sinai to Egypt. The canal reopened under Egyptian management in April of that year. Despite his military losses, Nasser was regarded in Egypt as a victor, and he became an Arab hero for standing up to the West.

The Suez crisis proved that the United States and the Soviet Union had become the leading powers in world politics.

After the Suez crisis, Arab guerrillas launched small-scale attacks inside Israel, and Israel responded with raids into Arab territory. At the same time, the Arab nationalist movement began receiving financial and military support from the Soviet Union. The United States, fearing the spread of Soviet-sponsored Communism, gave financial and military aid to Israel.

Birth of the PLO

In 1964, the Palestine Liberation Organization was formed to represent the Palestinian people. The PLO, a political body, is dedicated to defeating Israel and establishing an independent state for Palestinians in Palestine. Palestine today consists of Israel, the West Bank, and the Gaza Strip.

The Palestinians are an Arab group native to Palestine. There are about 12.5 million Palestinians. About 60 percent of them live outside Palestine. Many Palestinians—including many living in the West Bank and Gaza Strip—are refugees of Arab-Israeli wars or the descendants of refugees.

The PLO is an umbrella organization that includes guerrilla groups and associations of doctors, laborers, lawyers, women, students, and teachers. Some Palestinians are independent members of the PLO. Guerrilla groups, primarily Fatah (*FAH tah* or *fah TAH*), dominate the PLO.

The main branches of the PLO are the Palestine National Council (PNC), the Executive Committee, and the Central Council. The Palestine National Council serves as an assembly, or parliament, of the Palestinian people. The size of the PNC has varied over the years, but it generally has had a few hundred members. Some are elected, and others are appointed. The PNC is supposed to meet annually, but in some years, it does not meet. The PNC is the supreme authority of the PLO. It creates

Palestine Liberation Organization soldiers (above) were jubilant
after a military training exercise before the Six-Day War.
During the war, which began on June 5, 1967, and ended on June
10, Israel almost completely destroyed the air forces of Egypt
and other Arab countries.

policies, plans, and programs for the organization.

The Executive Committee is the PLO's highest executive body and
makes most day-to-day decisions. The PNC elects the chairman and the
other members of the Executive Committee. The chairman is the PLO's
highest official and has historically exercised great power over the
organization. The Central Council, which is also elected by the PNC,
meets on occasion to advise the Executive Committee.

Many Jews immigrated to Palestine during the 1900's. As Jewish
immigrants arrived, tensions developed between the Jews and the
Palestinians, who feared that the Jews would eventually dominate or

expel them. When, in 1948, the state of Israel was founded in the region as a homeland for Jews, war immediately broke out between Israel and Arab countries opposed to Israel's creation. Israel originally covered slightly more than half of Palestine. But because of the war, Israel gained additional territory, and numerous Palestinians were driven from areas under Israeli control. During the 1950's, some Palestinians began organizing resistance groups.

On Jan. 1, 1964, at an Arab summit meeting in Cairo, Egypt, Arab leaders called for the establishment of an organization to represent the

In early 1964, Arab leaders attending an Arab Summit Conference (above) in Cairo, Egypt, called for the establishment of an organization to represent the Palestinians. On May 28, 1964, the Palestine Liberation Organization was founded. Control of the PLO later fell into the hands of Palestinian guerrilla groups.

Palestinians. The leaders asked Ahmad al-Shuqayri *(AH mahd ahl shoo KAY ree)* (1908-1980), a Palestinian lawyer and diplomat, to nominate members for this organization. On May 28, 1964, al-Shuqayri's 422 Palestinian nominees met in Jerusalem. These delegates founded the Palestine Liberation Organization. Al-Shuqayri became the first chairman of the PLO Executive Committee.

After the 1967 war with Israel, control of the PLO fell into the hands of Palestinian guerrilla groups. The largest of these groups was Fatah, led by Yasir Arafat *(YAHS uhr AHR uh fat)* (1929-2004). In 1969, the Palestine National Council elected Arafat chairman of the PLO Executive Committee. Fatah and other guerrilla groups conducted numerous attacks and raids on Israeli targets. Israel, in turn, launched attacks against PLO and guerrilla sites. Arafat was head of the PLO until his death in 2004.

In 1993, the PLO and Israel conducted secret discussions in Oslo, Norway. The two sides reached an agreement that was signed on Sept. 13, 1993, in Washington, D.C. The agreement, the first of the so-called Oslo accords, called for the creation of a Palestinian Authority (PA) to manage the affairs of the Palestinians in the West Bank and Gaza Strip. The PLO continues to function as the representative of the Palestinian people. It is a member of the Arab League, an association of Arab states; has observer status at the United Nations; and maintains diplomatic relations with many countries. But with the creation of the PA, the PLO has lost some influence.

Six-Day War

In April 1967, a skirmish in Syria's Golan *(GOH lahn)* Heights led to an air battle between Israeli and Syrian warplanes. Egypt, pledging military support for Syria, demanded that the international United Nations

Emergency Force (UNEF troops) leave the Sinai *(SY ny)* Peninsula. During the 1957 Suez Canal crisis, the UNEF had taken positions around the canal, in Gaza, and in the Sinai.

Egyptian troops and tanks flooded into the peninsula. Egypt also blocked the Straits of Tiran in the Gulf of Aqaba *(AH kuh buh)* to Israeli shipping. The gulf was Israel's only access to the Red Sea. The blockage cut off the important Israeli port of Elat *(EE lat)*, also spelled Eilat *(ay LAHT)*, from the Red Sea, which Israel considered an act of war.

Syrian troops massed above the Israeli border in the Golan Heights, a hilly area covering 454 square miles (1,176 square kilometers) in the southwestern corner of the country bordering Israel. Most of its land is rocky, but a small part of it is fertile and supports agriculture.

By June 5, Egypt had signed defense agreements with Syria, Jordan, and Iraq, creating a joint military command.

Arab leaders—most notably Egyptian President Gamal Nasser—called for Israel's destruction. Some 330,000 Arab troops surrounded Israel, along with about 2,000 tanks and 600 warplanes. Israel's forces included about 250,000 troops, 1,000 tanks, and 250 warplanes. The Israelis were outnumbered, but they were better equipped, trained, and coordinated. After failed diplomatic efforts, Israel struck before the Arab forces could attack.

On June 5, Israel launched a surprise attack on Egypt. The Arab nations of Syria, Jordan, and Iraq joined Egypt in fighting Israel. Lebanon, Saudi Arabia, and other Arab nations played small roles in the conflict. Within hours, Israeli warplanes destroyed almost all the Arab air forces. Israeli warplanes struck several Egyptian air bases early that day, destroying hundreds of Egyptian planes. At the same time, Israeli tanks and infantry smashed into Gaza and the Sinai, routing Egyptian ground forces.

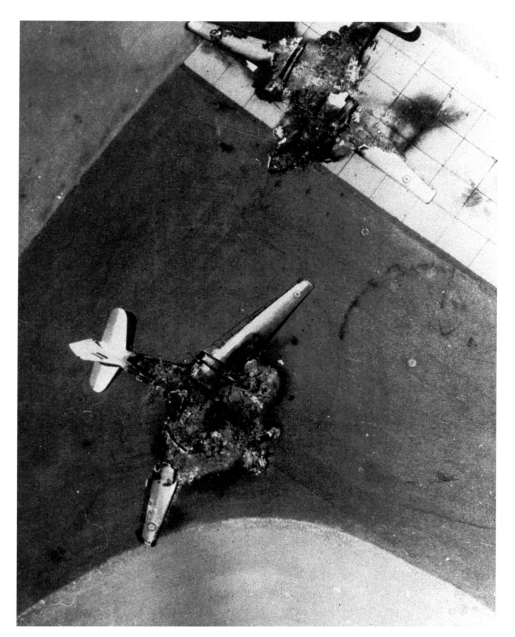

On June 5, 1967, Israel launched a surprise strike against Egyptian airfields at the start of the Six-Day War. The attack destroyed hundreds of Egyptian warplanes, including those shown above.

Ezer Weizman (1924-2005), the deputy chief of staff of the Israeli Defense Force, organized the strike against the Egyptian air force on the ground. Israeli tanks then retook the Sinai Peninsula. Israel also gained control of the West Bank, the Gaza Strip, and East Jerusalem. It had taken West Jerusalem in the 1948 war.

Late in the morning on June 5, Jordanian artillery and warplanes struck positions in northern Israel, including Tel Aviv *(TEHL uh VEEV)* and west Jerusalem. Israel responded with airstrikes that wiped out the Jordanian air force. That afternoon, Israeli troops began battling Jordanian forces in and around Jerusalem. Israeli warplanes destroyed Jordan's reinforcement convoys. By the morning of June 7, only pockets of Jordanian troops remained in Jerusalem. Israeli forces then entered and gained control of Jerusalem's walled Old City. By nightfall on June 7, Israel had taken the West Bank.

Syrian artillery and warplanes attacked Israeli targets along the Syrian border on June 5. Later that day, Israeli warplanes destroyed most of the Syrian air force. After fighting in the Sinai and the West Bank ended, Israel turned its attention to Syria's heavily defended Golan Heights. Early on June 9, Israeli warplanes battered Syrian troops entrenched on the heights. By noon, Israeli ground forces had entered Syria. Fierce battles erupted all along the border, but Israeli troops soon controlled the Golan Heights. A ceasefire on June 10 ended the Six-Day War.

About 800 Israelis died in the Six-Day War, and another 2,400 were wounded. Combined Arab *casualties* (people killed, wounded, missing, or captured) were about 50,000, including more than 14,000 dead.

During the Arab-Israeli war of 1967, the Suez Canal became blocked by sunken ships. Egypt did not reopen the canal until June 1975.

While Israelis call this conflict the Six-Day War, Arabs call it the June

In the 1967 Six-Day War, Israel faced the combined armies of Egypt, Jordan, and Syria. The fighting took place from June 5 to June 10 and ended in a decisive Israeli victory. At the war's conclusion, Israel occupied the West Bank, the Gaza Strip, the Sinai Peninsula, and the Golan Heights. The war's outcome led to further conflict and tensions in the Middle East.

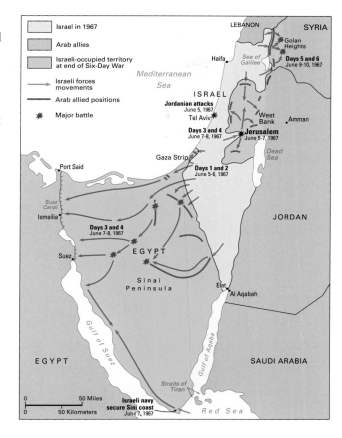

War. In November 1967, the UN called for Israel to withdraw from territories it gained in the war. In return, the Arab countries were to recognize and accept the nation of Israel's right to exist. However, Israel refused to give up the captured territories, and the Arab countries renewed their opposition to Israel.

While Israel would eventually return the Sinai Peninsula and leave the Gaza Strip, it still occupies the Golan Heights and parts of the West Bank. In 1981, Israel claimed legal and political authority in the Golan Heights. But Syria rejects this claim, and many other countries do not recognize it, since the Golan Height has been considered Syrian territory since ancient times.

Also after the 1967 war, the PLO sought to become the representative of the Palestinians in world politics. It developed educational and social service organizations for Palestinians, mainly in the West Bank and Gaza Strip and in refugee camps in Lebanon and Jordan.

The PLO also began to take independent military action. In the late 1960's, PLO groups began to attack Israelis both inside and outside Israel. In response, Israel attacked Palestinian refugee camps in Jordan and Lebanon, in which many guerrillas were based. The Israelis also assassinated several PLO leaders.

The 1972 Summer Games were held in Munich, in what was then West Germany. The Munich Olympics are remembered for the events of September 5. Eight Palestinian terrorists broke into the Olympic Village and entered the dormitory of the Israeli team. They killed two Israelis and took nine hostages, demanding the release of more than 200 Arab prisoners in Israel. During a battle with West German sharpshooters, all the Israeli hostages were killed, along with five terrorists and one policeman.

Four years after the Israeli hostage situation at the Munich Summer Olympics, Palestinian terrorists again targeted Israelis in hijacking a French airplane and forcing the pilot to land at Entebbe (*ehn TEHB ay*), a major city in Uganda that lies on Lake Victoria's northwest shore and south of the Ugandan capital of Kampala. They held over 100 of the passengers—chiefly Israeli citizens—as hostages. A week later, Israeli commandos staged a daring raid at the airport, freeing almost all the hostages. Like the Munich Olympic hostage crisis, a deadly showdown also ensued in this raid. Three hostages were killed in crossfire between the commandos, terrorists, and Ugandan soldiers.

After the 1967 war, Egyptian and Israeli troops continued to attack each other across the western border of the Sinai Peninsula. Egypt and Syria still refused to accept Israel's existence and demanded that Israel return the territories it gained in the war—Jordan's West Bank, Syria's Golan Heights, and Egypt's Gaza Strip and Sinai Peninsula. Israel refused, and Egypt and Syria again prepared for war.

Yom Kippur War

After the 1967 war, Israel built strong defenses east of the Suez Canal, which separates mainland Egypt from the Sinai Peninsula. In the

The Arab-Israeli conflict erupted into war in June 1967. Israeli forces (shown here advancing on the Golan Heights) defeated Egypt, Syria, and Jordan in the Six-Day War. Israel seized the Sinai Peninsula and the Gaza Strip from Egypt, the Golan Heights from Syria, and the West Bank (including East Jerusalem) from Jordan. Israel later returned the Sinai Peninsula to Egypt.

autumn of 1973, Egypt had about 600,000 active troops, 2,200 tanks, and 550 aircraft. Many thousands of Egyptian troops secretly massed on the Suez Canal's west bank. At the same time, Syria gathered 1,400 tanks and about 120,000 troops near the Golan Heights. Intent on recovering lost land, Egypt and Syria chose the combined holidays of Yom Kippur (*YOHM kih POOR*) and Ramadan (*ram uh DAHN* or *rahm uh DAHN*) to launch simultaneous attacks.

Israel's forces included some 350,000 troops, 2,000 tanks, and 480 warplanes. However, only a few thousand troops were on active duty in the Sinai Peninsula or near the Golan Heights. After fighting began, Israel had to quickly call up reserves, dividing them between the two fronts. The Israelis were outnumbered, but they continued to be better equipped, trained, and coordinated. The United States supplied Israel with large amounts of military equipment, which gave the Israelis a boost.

On Oct. 6, 1973, Egypt and Syria launched a massive assault on Israeli forces in the Sinai Peninsula and Golan Heights, starting the fourth major Arab-Israeli conflict since the nation of Israel was established in 1948. The attack took Israel by surprise, in part because it came on Yom Kippur, the holiest day in Judaism. Israeli defenders, surprised and outnumbered, were overrun or surrounded.

At first, Egypt drove Israel's forces out of the western Sinai, and Syria pushed Israeli troops from the eastern Golan Heights. The Egyptians then pressed forward against Israeli counterattacks. After days of bloody fighting for limited gains, the Egyptian advance stopped.

On October 14, Israeli forces drove back a massive Egyptian tank attack. Some 250 Egyptian tanks were destroyed. Israeli forces counter-attacked, dividing the Egyptian forces. Israeli troops crossed the Suez Canal and advanced into Egypt. After bitter fighting farther north,

Israeli troops also regained much of the area lost days earlier.

The United Nations arranged a cease-fire on October 22, but fighting between the two nations continued. The two sides officially obeyed a second UN cease-fire on October 24. By then, Israeli forces had surrounded the Egyptian army. They also defeated the Syrian army in the Golan Heights. Israelis call this war the Yom Kippur War. Arabs call it the October War or the Ramadan War since the conflict occurred during the month of Ramadan, a Muslim holy month.

In fighting on the Golan Heights front during the war, the outnumbered Israeli troops initially fell back against Syrian forces. But after quick reinforcement, the Israelis stopped the Syrian advance. At great

On Oct. 6, 1973, Egypt and Syria launched a surprise assault on Israeli forces in the Sinai Peninsula and the Golan Heights. By October 24, Israeli forces had surrounded the Egyptian army and defeated the Syrian army in the Yom Kippur War. Israeli tanks are shown above in the Golan Heights.

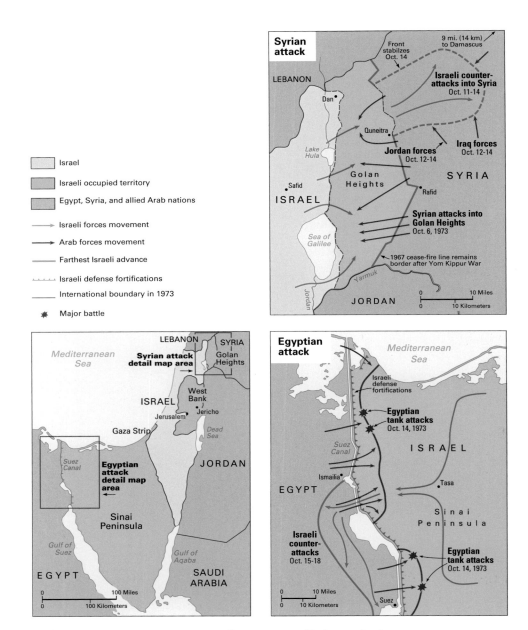

In the 1973 Yom Kippur War, Israeli troops repelled attacks from both Egypt and Syria. The war ended in a stalemate, but it led to important changes in Arab-Israeli relations in the Middle East.

cost to both sides, Israeli forces then drove the Syrians from the Golan Heights and advanced into Syria. Aided by Iraqi and Jordanian troops, the Syrians finally stopped the Israelis about 25 miles (40 kilometers) from Damascus, the Syrian capital.

The first UN ceasefire on October 22 largely ended the fighting in Syria. As in Egypt, occasional violence continued for months. Israel and Syria agreed to an armistice on May 31, 1974.

More than 2,500 Israeli soldiers died in the Yom Kippur War, and more than 7,000 were wounded. Combined Arab casualties surpassed 50,000, including some 12,000 to 15,000 dead.

The Yom Kippur War had far-reaching effects on Israel. The heavy loss of men, as well as equipment, hit the country hard. The Israeli economy suffered severely. Many Israelis criticized the government's handling of the conflict. As a result, Prime Minister Golda Meir (*may EER*) (1898-1978) resigned in April 1974. Yitzhak Rabin succeeded her in June. The war also greatly increased Israel's dependence on the United States, which supplied Israel with arms. The Yom Kippur War eventually led to agreements made in the 1978 Camp David Accords.

Israel had fought four wars with Arab nations in a span of 28 years. While Israeli forces gained success on Middle Eastern battlefronts and gained territory, the periodic conflicts took a toll on the country. Palestinian leaders organized through the PLO to advocate for their people and territory. Also, Palestine allied with Arab nations, which maintained opposition to the existence of Israel. The willingness of Arab nations to antagonize Israel would be tested by the 1978 Camp David Accords between leaders of Israel and Egypt. Even though the accords only settled issues between those two countries, they opened the door for future peace processes. Peace deals were reached between Israel and Palestine. Still, fighting persisted.

Israeli Prime Minister Menachem Begin (shown here) shared the 1978 Nobel Peace Prize with Egyptian President Anwar el-Sadat for their efforts to end the Arab-Israeli conflict.

CHAPTER FIVE

Important figures in the conflict

Menachem Begin

Menachem Begin *(mehn AHK hehm BAY guhn)* (1913-1992) served as prime minister of Israel from 1977 to 1983. The leader of the conservative Likud *(lih KOOD)* Party, he came to power after the party won most of the seats in the *Knesset* (Israeli parliament). After the 1981 elections, the Likud Party and smaller conservative parties formed a coalition and Begin remained prime minister. Begin resigned from office in 1983.

In 1978, Begin, President Anwar el-Sadat of Egypt, and U.S. President Jimmy Carter held discussions in the United States about ways to end the Arab-Israeli conflict, which resulted in a major agreement (the Camp David Accords) that included plans for Israel's withdrawal from the Sinai Peninsula and called for a peace treaty between Israel and Egypt. Begin and Sadat shared the 1978 Nobel Peace Prize for their efforts to end the Arab-Israeli conflict. The treaty was signed in 1979. Israel's withdrawal from the Sinai Peninsula was completed in 1982.

In 1981, Begin's government claimed legal and political authority over the Golan Heights, which Israel had seized in the Six-Day War against Syria in 1967. Syria and many other countries denounced this claim. Although Israel's relations with Egypt improved under Begin, relations with other Arab countries remained hostile.

Begin was born on Aug. 16, 1913, in Brest-Litovsk, Russia (now Brest, Belarus). In the 1930's, he became active in the Zionist movement. The

Zionists called for the creation of a Jewish nation in Palestine, which was then ruled by the British. Begin moved to Palestine in 1942. There he joined the Irgun Zvai Leumi *(EER gun zvy lay OO mee),* an underground Jewish militia that fought the British and Palestinian Arabs. Begin led the Irgun from 1944 to 1948, when the nation of Israel was created in Palestine. He played a leading military role in the Arab-Israeli war of 1948. Begin served in the Knesset from 1949 to 1984. He died on March 9, 1992.

Anwar el-Sadat

Anwar el-Sadat *(AHN wahr ehl suh DAHT)* (1918-1981) was president of Egypt from 1970 until his death in 1981. Under his leadership, Egypt negotiated with Israel to end the long-standing conflict between the two countries. Sadat gained admiration throughout much of the world for his peacemaking efforts. But many Arabs in Egypt and elsewhere severely criticized him. Sadat was assassinated on Oct. 6, 1981, by Egyptian militants who opposed his harsh policies against his own people.

Sadat became president in 1970 after the death of President Gamal Abdel Nasser. Sadat broke Egypt's ties with the Soviet Union and worked to develop better relations with the United States. Sadat also demanded the return of Egypt's Sinai Peninsula, which Israel had occupied in 1967. In 1973, Egypt and Syria began a war (the Yom Kippur War) with Israel to try to regain Israeli-occupied territories. The Arab states failed. But Sadat's attack against Israeli occupation raised his popularity among Arabs and drew U.S. attention to the need for Middle East stability.

After the war, Sadat's government reached agreements with Israel under which Israeli troops withdrew from parts of the Sinai. In 1977, Sadat made a historic trip to Israel and addressed the Knesset.

In 1978, Sadat and Israeli Prime Minister Menachem Begin met in the

Egyptian President Anwar el-Sadat held office from 1970 until he was assassinated on Oct. 6, 1981. Sadat gained admiration throughout much of the world for his peacemaking efforts. He is shown here during a state visit to the United States in August 1981.

United States for talks arranged by U.S. President Jimmy Carter. The discussions resulted in the Camp David Accords, a major agreement that included plans for Israel's withdrawal from all of the Sinai. The agreement also called for an Israel-Egypt peace treaty.

Sadat and Begin shared the 1978 Nobel Peace Prize for their efforts. A peace treaty was signed in 1979. Israel completed its withdrawal from the Sinai in 1982.

Sadat's treaty with Israel was extremely unpopular in the Arab world, mainly because Egypt failed to resolve the conflict's main issue—the Palestinian struggle against Israel. In 1981, Sadat cracked down on his political opposition in Egypt by ordering the arrest of about 1,600

Egyptian President Anwar el-Sadat's coffin, draped with the red, white, and black Egyptian flag, is carried on a horse-drawn caisson during a funeral procession to be buried at Egypt's Tomb of the Unknown Soldier. The pyramid-shaped tomb (shown here in the background) is located in the Nasr City district of Cairo, Egypt.

people. Shortly afterward, he was assassinated in Cairo, on October 6, when gunmen taking part in a military parade opened fire on him.

Sadat was born on Dec. 25, 1918, in a village in the Nile River Delta. He graduated from the Egyptian Military Academy in 1938. He then joined Nasser and other young army officers in a group that worked to overthrow the government and rid Egypt of British troops. Sadat was imprisoned in the 1940's for his activities. In 1952, he helped lead the revolt that overthrew King Faruk. Sadat held a series of government positions after the uprising. He was vice president of Egypt from 1964 to 1967 and from 1969 to 1970.

Yitzhak Rabin

Yitzhak Rabin *(YIHTS hahk rah BEEN)* (1922-1995) was prime minister of Israel from 1974 to 1977 and from 1992 until his death. On Nov. 4, 1995, he was assassinated in Tel Aviv, Israel. A right-wing Israeli university student who opposed Rabin's policies confessed to the murder.

Rabin was born in Jerusalem and was the nation's first prime minister born in Israel. Israel's previous prime ministers were born in Europe. In 1941, during World War II, Rabin joined the *Palmach (pahl MAHK),* a unit of the Jewish underground army in Palestine. He was deputy commander of the Palmach in 1948 during the first Arab-Israeli war.

Rabin headed Israel's defense forces from 1964 to 1967. He planned the strategy in the 1967 Six-Day War in which the Israelis defeated the Arabs and occupied the Arab lands of the Gaza Strip and West Bank.

From 1968 to 1973, Rabin was Israel's ambassador to the United States. A Labor Party member, he was elected to Israel's parliament in 1973. He became Labor Party head and prime minister in 1974 and held those posts until 1977. He was minister of defense from 1984 to 1990.

Rabin again became Labor Party head in February 1992. Elections in

U.S. President Bill Clinton (center) looks on as Israeli Prime Minister Yitzhak Rabin (left) and PLO Chairman Yasir Arafat (right) shake hands after signing the Mideast peace accord at the White House in September 1993.

June brought the party to power, and Rabin became prime minister again. He appointed himself minister of defense. In 1993, Rabin's government and the Palestine Liberation Organization signed an agreement that included the start of a plan for self-government for, and Israel's withdrawal from, the Gaza Strip and West Bank. Israel and the PLO also agreed to try to work out their conflicts.

Rabin, Israeli foreign minister Shimon Peres, and PLO leader Yasir Arafat shared the 1994 Nobel Peace Prize for their peace efforts. Also in

1994, talks between Rabin and King Hussein I of Jordan led to a peace treaty ending a state of war that had technically existed between their countries since 1948.

Shimon Peres

Shimon Peres *(shih MOHN PEH rehs)* (1923-2016) was president of Israel from 2007 to 2014. He also served as prime minister twice—first from 1984 to 1986 and again in 1995 following the assassination of Prime Minister Yitzhak Rabin. In 1996, Benjamin Netanyahu *(neh tahn YAH hoo)* (1949-   ) replaced him as prime minister.

In the early and mid-1990's, both as foreign minister under Prime Minister Yitzhak Rabin and as prime minister himself, Peres played a major role in a move for peace between Israel and the PLO. Peres, Rabin, and PLO leader Yasir Arafat shared the 1994 Nobel Peace Prize for their Middle East peace efforts.

Peres served as prime minister in the unity government created by the Labor Party and the Likud bloc in September 1984. The parties formed the government after no party won a majority in the parliamentary elections. The unity government lasted for 50 months. Under the agreement between Labor and Likud, Peres—head of the Labor Party—served as prime minister for 25 months. Yitzhak Shamir *(YIHTS zhahk shah MEER)* (1915-2012), head of Likud, was vice prime minister and foreign minister. Under the agreement, the roles of Peres and Shamir were reversed after 25 months—in October 1986.

As prime minister, Peres pledged to withdraw Israeli troops that occupied Lebanon. The troops had invaded Lebanon in 1982. In 1985, the Israeli forces withdrew from all of Lebanon except a Security Zone along the Israeli border.

In 1988, Labor and Likud formed a new coalition government with

Shamir as prime minister. Peres remained as vice prime minister and also became finance minister. In 1990, the coalition collapsed, and Peres resigned from his posts as vice prime minister and finance minister. Likud and small parties formed a new coalition government with Shamir as prime minister. Peres had become head of the Labor Party in 1977. In 1992, he lost that post in a party election. He again served as Labor Party leader from 1995 to 1997 and from 2003 to 2005. In 2005, Peres was deputy prime minister in a coalition government headed by Prime Minister Ariel Sharon *(ah ree EHL shah ROHN)* of Likud.

Peres was born on Aug. 16, 1923, in Vishnevo, a small town near Minsk, that was then part of Poland and is now part of Belarus. His family name was Persky. He changed the name to Peres in the 1940's. Peres moved with his family to Palestine in 1934. He later became active in the movement that resulted in the creation of the nation of Israel in Palestine in 1948.

In 1950, Peres was sent to the United States as leader of a defense ministry delegation. While there, he studied at New York University and Harvard University. He returned to Israel in 1952.

Peres was first elected to the Israeli Knesset in 1959. He helped form the Labor Party in 1968. He was minister of defense from 1974 to 1977. He served as foreign minister in 1987 and 1988, from 1992 to 1995, and in 2001 and 2002. Peres joined the Kadima *(kah DEE mah)* party in 2005. He died on Sept. 28, 2016.

Ezer Weizman

Ezer Weizman (1924-2005), an Israeli political and military leader, was president of Israel from 1993 to 2000. His role as president was largely ceremonial, and he played a limited role in Israeli politics. Weizman's political views changed during his political career. He initially favored

Shimon Peres served as both president and prime minister of Israel. He shared the 1994 Nobel Peace Prize with Yitzhak Rabin and Yasir Arafat.

Important figures in the conflict   87

the anti-Arab policies of Israel's right-wing parties, supporting the Likud Front in its election victory in 1977. After he took part in Israel's peace negotiations with Egypt in the late 1970's, however, Weizman supported increased relations with the Arab states. He supported more open Israeli-Arab relations through the rest of his political career.

Weizman was born on June 15, 1924, in Tel Aviv. He was the nephew of Chaim Weizmann, one of the architects of the modern Zionist movement and the first president of Israel. At age 18, Ezer Weizman joined the Royal Air Force (RAF) and served in Egypt, which was under the control of the United Kingdom at that time. He became a fighter pilot and served in India in World War II.

During the 1948 Arab-Israeli War, Weizman was a member of the Israeli Air Force (IAF). He became head of the IAF in 1958 and continued in the service until 1966. In that year, he became deputy to Yitzhak Rabin, the chief of staff of the Israel Defense Force (IDF), who later became prime minister. In the June 1967 Six-Day War, Weizman organized a strike by Israeli fighters against the Egyptian air force on the ground. The strike allowed Israel to win a rapid and decisive victory over the Arab forces.

In 1969, Weizman resigned from the military and entered politics. He held the posts of minister of transportation in 1969 and 1970 and minister of defense from 1977 to 1980. He resigned from the government in 1980 and worked in private business until he returned to politics in 1984 as a Labor Party minister.

Weizman was minister of communications from 1984 to 1988 and minister of science from 1988 to 1992. He resigned in 1992 over charges that he had had secret, unauthorized meetings with a member of the Palestine Liberation Organization, the political body that represents Palestinians.

Ezer Weizman served as president of Israel from 1993 to 2000. However, his role was largely ceremonial. Weizman resigned as president following allegations he illegally accepted cash gifts while in office.

In 1993, Weizman was elected president by the Knesset. He was re-elected in 1998 to a five-year term.

In January 2000, Israeli police launched an investigation into allegations that Weizman illegally accepted cash gifts while serving as president. The Israeli attorney general found that Weizman acted improperly, but no charges were filed. Weizman resigned as president in July 2000. Weizman died on April 24, 2005.

Ariel Sharon

Ariel Sharon (1928-2014) was prime minister of Israel from 2001 to 2006. Sharon, nicknamed "Arik," was known for many years as a critic of the Oslo peace process between Israel and the Palestinians. Throughout most of his career, he was a strong supporter of Jewish settlements in the West Bank and Gaza Strip, territories that Israel occupied in 1967.

Sharon was born in 1928, probably on February 27, in Kfar Malal, a Jewish cooperative farming settlement near Tel Aviv in what was then Palestine. His original name was Ariel Scheinerman, but he later adopted the name Sharon. As a teenager, he joined an underground Jewish defense force that had been set up to protect Jewish settlers from Arab raiding parties.

From 1948 to 1973, he served in the Israel Defense Force, where he rose through the ranks. He became a major general in 1967. He fought in the Israeli war of independence in 1948, the Sinai campaign of 1956, the Six-Day War of 1967, and the Yom Kippur War of 1973. Among some people, he gained a reputation for bravery. Others, particularly Palestinians, considered him ruthless.

In 1973, Sharon entered politics. He helped form Likud to challenge the Labor Party's control of the Knesset. He was elected to the Knesset, but he resigned in 1974. In 1975, he became an adviser to Israeli Prime

Ariel Sharon was prime minister of Israel from 2001 to 2006. Among some people, Sharon gained a reputation for bravery. Others, particularly Palestinians, considered him ruthless.

Important figures in the conflict   91

Minister Yitzhak Rabin. In 1977, Sharon was again elected to the Knesset. He held many Cabinet posts, including minister of agriculture in charge of settlements from 1977 to 1981 and minister of defense from 1981 to 1983.

As defense minister, Sharon directed the Israeli invasion of Lebanon in June 1982. The invasion was primarily a response to attacks on northern Israel by PLO forces based in southern Lebanon. Sharon was criticized for extending the invasion north into Beirut, the Lebanese capital, as well as failing to prevent a massacre of hundreds of Palestinian civilians in September 1982 by Lebanese Christian militia forces in the Israeli-occupied part of Beirut. Sharon was forced to resign as defense minister in February 1983 after an Israeli commission declared him indirectly responsible for the incident. Sharon went on to serve in other Cabinet roles.

In 1999, Sharon was elected chairman of Likud. In September 2000, he made a controversial visit to the Temple Mount in Jerusalem. The Temple Mount, known to Muslims as Haram al-Sharif *(hah RAHM ahl shah REEF)*, is a holy site for both Jews and Muslims. At the time, disagreements regarding who should govern the site were stalling peace talks between Israel and the Palestinians. Sharon's visit led to violence between Palestinian protesters and Israeli troops in Israel, the West Bank, and the Gaza Strip.

The violence led Israeli Prime Minister Ehud Barak *(eh HOOD buh RAHK)* to call a special election for prime minister. In the 2001 election, Sharon defeated Barak. Parliamentary elections in January 2003 gave Likud the largest number of seats in the Knesset. Sharon remained prime minister.

In 2004, Sharon announced a plan to remove Jewish settlements and Israeli troops from the Gaza Strip and four West Bank settlements. In

August 2005, the settlers were evacuated, and the last Israeli troops left in September. Many Likud members had opposed the plan, and the party began to split. In late 2005, Sharon asked for early elections. He left Likud and formed a moderate party called Kadima *(kah DEE mah),* which is Hebrew for *forward.*

In January 2006, Sharon suffered a major stroke and fell into a coma. Deputy Prime Minister Ehud Olmert *(eh HOOD OHL mehrt)* (1945-   ) became acting prime minister and acting head of Kadima. Parliamentary elections were held in March 2006, and Kadima won the largest number of seats. Olmert, as head of Kadima, became prime minister. Sharon died on Jan. 11, 2014.

Yasir Arafat

Yasir Arafat (1929-2004) was head of the Palestine Liberation Organization from 1969 to 2004 and president of the Palestinian Authority from 1996 to 2004. (His first name is also spelled Yasser.) The Palestine Liberation Organization is a political body that represents the Palestinian people. The PLO's goal is to establish an independent Palestinian state in the West Bank and Gaza Strip, territories fully or partly occupied by Israel since 1967.

Arafat probably was born on Aug. 24, 1929, in Cairo, Egypt, to Palestinian parents. He claimed that he was born in Jerusalem. His full name was Mohammed Abdel-Raouf Arafat al-Qudwa al-Husseini. He acquired the nickname Yasir, which means *easygoing,* as a teenager. In 1956, he earned a degree in civil engineering at King Fuad I University (later Cairo University).

In the 1950's, Arafat helped organize Fatah, a guerrilla group that opposed Israeli control of territory in Palestine. In 1964, Arab leaders established the PLO to represent the Palestinians. In 1967, Israel defeated Arab countries in the Six-Day War and occupied the West Bank and Gaza Strip. After the war, Palestinian guerrilla groups gained control of the PLO. The largest guerrilla group was Fatah, led by Arafat. In 1969, Arafat was elected chairman of the PLO Executive Committee, the highest PLO post. Fatah and other PLO groups repeatedly raided and attacked Israeli targets and, in turn, Israel attacked PLO and guerrilla bases.

In 1974, Arafat became the first person to address the United Nations General Assembly as a leader of a liberation movement rather than a UN member country. That year, the UN recognized the PLO as the representative of the Palestinians.

In 1982, Israel invaded Lebanon, where the PLO was based. Arafat and his supporters were forced to leave their bases in Lebanon. They then moved to Tunisia in northern Africa.

In 1993, the PLO and Israel agreed to the creation of a Palestinian Authority to govern Palestinian-controlled parts of the West Bank and Gaza Strip. The Palestinian Authority was founded in 1994.

In the 1990's, Israeli-PLO agreements led to the withdrawal of Israeli troops from most of the Gaza Strip and many cities and towns of the West Bank. As the Israelis withdrew, the PA took control of these areas. In 1994, Arafat moved to the Gaza Strip, marking the end of a 27-year exile from Palestine. That year, Arafat and the Israeli leaders Yitzhak Rabin and Shimon Peres shared the Nobel Peace Prize for their peace efforts. In 1996, Arafat was elected president of the PA.

In 2000, peace talks between Israel and the PLO broke down, and a period of violence began between Israelis and Palestinians. Arafat's position was weakened. In 2003, he agreed to appoint a prime minister to assume some of his PA executive duties. In late 2004, Arafat became seriously ill. He died on Nov. 11, 2004.

Yasir Arafat was leader of the Palestine Liberation Organization from 1969 until his death in 2004. He was also president of the Palestinian Authority from 1996 to 2004.

Mahmoud Abbas

Mahmoud Abbas *(mah MOOD ah BAHS)* (1935-   ), also known as Abu Mazen, is the head of the Palestine Liberation Organization and the president of the Palestinian Authority. (His first name is sometimes spelled Mahmud.)

Abbas is chairman of the PLO Executive Committee, the organization's highest executive body. He assumed the chairmanship in November 2004, following the death of Yasir Arafat, who had served as chairman since 1969. Before becoming chairman, Abbas served as secretary-general of the Executive Committee.

Abbas is widely regarded as a moderate politician. He is known for his efforts to find a peaceful solution to the conflict between Israel and the Palestinians. In 1993, Abbas was part of a Palestinian delegation that held secret talks with Israeli officials in Oslo, Norway. These talks led to the signing of a peace agreement in September 1993, the first of several agreements in what has become known as the Oslo peace process. This process continued through the 1990's, but some key issues have not yet been resolved, and violence between Israelis and Palestinians has caused interruptions since 2000.

Abbas was born in 1935 in Zefat *(zeh VAHT),* also called Safad or Safed, in an area of Palestine that is now northern Israel. During the war that occurred after the state of Israel was established in 1948, Abbas sought refuge in Syria with his family. He became involved with the Palestinian independence movement in the 1950's. During that time, Abbas and Yasir Arafat helped found the Palestinian guerrilla group Fatah, which later became part of the PLO.

In 1958, Abbas earned a bachelor's degree in law from the University of Damascus in Syria. In 1980, he became head of the PLO's national and

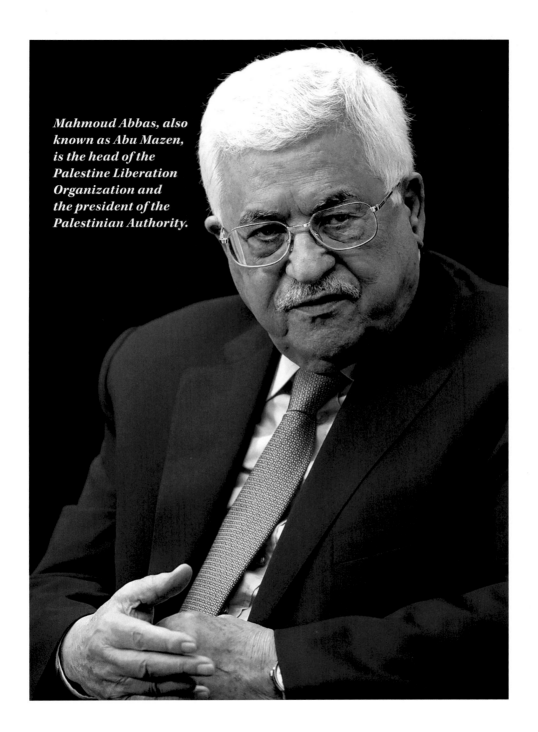

Mahmoud Abbas, also known as Abu Mazen, is the head of the Palestine Liberation Organization and the president of the Palestinian Authority.

international relations department. In 1982, he earned a doctorate in history from the Institute of Oriental Studies in Moscow.

Abbas returned to live in Palestine in 1995 for the first time since he went into exile in 1948. He became secretary-general of the PLO Executive Committee in 1996. From April to September 2003, Abbas served as the first prime minister of the Palestinian Authority. Arafat had allowed the post of prime minister to be created earlier that year in response to international pressure to give up some of his power. In January 2005, Abbas was elected president of the Palestinian Authority by a wide margin. He replaced Arafat, who had served as Palestinian Authority president from 1996 until his death.

Hussein I

Hussein (*hoo SAYN*) I (1935-1999) was king of Jordan from 1952 to 1999. He became known for his efforts to achieve peace between Arabs and Israelis in the Middle East. He also led efforts to develop Jordan's economy. Hussein was a member of Jordan's Hashemite (*HASH uh myt*) *dynasty* (family of rulers). This family, the Hashemites, traces its ancestry back to Muhammad, the prophet whose life and teachings form the basis of Islam.

Hussein was born on Nov. 14, 1935, in Amman, the capital city of Jordan (then called Transjordan). In 1951, a Palestinian gunman shot Jordan's King Abdullah I (1882-1951), Hussein's grandfather, in Jerusalem. The gunman also fired at Hussein, who was standing near the king. According to Hussein's autobiography, a bullet bounced off a medal on Hussein's chest.

Hussein attended Victoria College in Egypt and Harrow College and the Royal Military Academy in England. He married Dina Abdul Hamed in 1955, but the couple divorced the following year. Hussein was married

Hussein I was king of Jordan from 1952 to 1999. His family traces its ancestry back to the prophet Muhammad, whose teachings form the basis of Islam.

Important figures in the conflict   99

U.S. President Bill Clinton (center) stands by as Israeli Prime Minister Yitzhak Rabin (left) shakes hands with Jordan's King Hussein I after signing a historic peace deal in October 1994. The deal formally ended a state of war that existed between Israel and Jordan since 1948.

to his second wife, Princess Muna al-Hussein (born Toni Gardiner), from 1961 to 1972. He married Alia Baha Eddin Toukan, his third wife, in 1972, but she died in 1977 when the military helicopter she was riding in crashed in a rainstorm in southern Jordan. Hussein married Queen Noor (born Lisa Halaby) in 1978. He had five sons and six daughters.

Hussein succeeded his father, Talal, as king in 1952. In 1967, Jordan, Egypt, and Syria were defeated by Israel in the Six-Day War. Israel occupied part of western Jordan, an area in Palestine called the West Bank. As a result, many West Bank Palestinians fled to eastern Jordan. Eventually, Palestinian guerrillas threatened to overthrow Hussein. His stand against them led to a civil war between Jordanian and Palestinian forces in 1970. The Jordanians quickly won the war. In 1974, Hussein gave up Jordan's authority over the West Bank but continued to give it financial and administrative support. In 1988, he ended Jordan's support of the West Bank.

In 1990, Iraq invaded and occupied Kuwait. Western and Arab countries formed an alliance and drove Iraq out of Kuwait in 1991. Hussein remained neutral in the conflict. As a result, Jordan's relations with Arab countries in the alliance became strained.

In July 1994, Hussein and Israeli Prime Minister Yitzhak Rabin agreed to end a state of war that had technically existed between Jordan and Israel since 1948. The two nations signed a historic peace treaty in October 1994.

Hussein became a leader in efforts to bring peace to the Middle East. In 1998, for example, though ill with cancer, he helped negotiate an agreement between the Israelis and the Palestinians.

Hussein died on Feb. 7, 1999. Abdullah II (*ab DUHL uh* or *ab dool LAH*) (1962-   ), the oldest son of Hussein and Princess Muna al-Hussein, succeeded him.

In 1978, U.S. President Jimmy Carter (center) hosted a peace summit with Israeli leader Menachem Begin (left) and Eygptian leader Anwar el-Sadat (right) at the U.S. presidential retreat at Camp David in the state of Maryland.

CHAPTER SIX

Peace accords and continued conflict

T he Labor Party and the party from which it developed, the Mapai, controlled Israel's government from independence until 1977. Under Israel's political system of the time, the prime minister was usually the leader of the party with the most seats in the Knesset. In 1977, parliamentary elections transferred control of the country to the Likud bloc, a conservative party comprising several smaller groups. Menachem Begin, the Likud leader, became prime minister. Even though the Likud bloc has often opposed compromise in Israel's conflict with Palestinians and other Arabs of the Middle East, its attitude had warmed in the late 1970's as Israeli-Egyptian tensions eased after the Yom Kippur War.

Camp David Accords

In November 1977, Egyptian President Anwar el-Sadat announced that he was ready to negotiate a peace settlement with Israel. That month, he met with Begin in Jerusalem.

In September 1978, Sadat joined Begin and U.S. President Jimmy Carter (1924-   ) in signing the Camp David Accords. Carter arranged meetings with Sadat and Begin at Camp David, a U.S. presidential retreat in the state of Maryland, to work out the accords. Under these agreements, Egypt recognized Israel's right to exist. In return, Israel agreed to give back to Egypt the part of the Sinai it still occupied. Israel had returned the far western part of the Sinai in 1975. Sadat and Begin also agreed there was a need for national independence for the Palestinians. In talks leading up to the accords, Egypt and Israel received promises of large amounts of U.S. economic and military aid. In 1979, Egypt and Israel signed a treaty that confirmed their new peaceful relationship. In 1980, they exchanged diplomats for the first time. Israel completed its withdrawal from Egypt's Sinai Peninsula in 1982.

While the Camp David Accords made peace between Egypt and Israel, it did not make immediate progress on a broader objective, a comprehensive peace in the Middle East.

The Camp David Accords became one of Carter's signature foreign policy achievements, but the treaty was unpopular in the Arab world. Most Arab leaders strongly opposed the Camp David Accords and the 1979 treaty. As a result, Egypt was expelled from the Arab League in 1979. In 1981, Sadat was assassinated by an Egyptian religious group that opposed his policies.

Tensions between Israel and the PLO escalated in the late 1970's and early 1980's. In 1978, Israel invaded southern Lebanon to drive out Palestinian guerrillas based there who had been attacking Israel for several years. The PLO continued to launch guerrilla attacks on Israel from Lebanon. In June 1982, a large Israeli force invaded Lebanon and drove the PLO out of the southern part of the country by August. In 1985, Israel withdrew its forces from all of Lebanon except a security zone along the Lebanon-Israeli border. Israeli forces remained there until 2000.

The intifada

In 1987, Palestinians in the West Bank and Gaza Strip began an uprising against Israel's military rule of those territories. During this *intifada (ihn tih FAH dah)*, demonstrations occurred throughout the occupied

Tensions between Israel and the PLO escalated in the late 1970's and early 1980's. Israel invaded southern Lebanon in 1978 and again in 1982 to drive out Palestinian guerrillas who had been attacking Israel from Lebanon. This image shows Israeli tanks rumbling toward Lebanon.

territories. (*Intifada* is an Arabic term meaning *uprising* or *shaking off*.) Entire towns refused to pay taxes to Israel. Palestinians quit their jobs with Israeli employers. Most demonstrations were peaceful, but a few became violent. The intifada grabbed international attention and triggered criticism of Israel for its continuing control of the West Bank and Gaza Strip and for its extensive use of force in trying to control the Palestinians.

The Islamic Jihad of Palestine (*ihs LAH mihk,* or *ihz LAH mihk, jih HAHD uhv PAL uh styn*), a radical Palestinian group, carried out one of its first attacks during the first intifada, the killing of an Israeli military police captain in the Gaza Strip.

In 1987, Palestinians in the West Bank and Gaza Strip began an uprising against Israeli military rule of those territories. Violence by both sides killed hundreds of Israelis and thousands of Palestinians. Israeli soldiers are shown above firing at stone-throwing Palestinian teenagers in the Gaza Strip.

The Islamic Jihad of Palestine does not recognize Israel's right to exist and seeks to establish an Islamic state in the historic region of Palestine. The group was founded around 1980 by Fathi Shiqaqi (*FAHT hee shuh KAH kee*) and a few other Palestinians after being inspired by the 1979 revolution in Iran that turned that country into an Islamic republic. Islamic Jihad is much smaller than Hamas (*hah MAHS*). Like Hamas, Islamic Jihad has carried out suicide bombings and other terrorist attacks against Israeli military and civilian targets. The two groups have often worked together.

The first intifada began in December 1987 and lasted until 1993. The second intifada ran from September 2000 to 2005. Israeli forces had captured the West Bank and the Gaza Strip, the two Palestinian territories, in June 1967, during the Six-Day War.

The first intifada consisted mainly of strikes, marches, boycotts, and other nonviolent resistance. Some Palestinians threw stones and gasoline bombs at Israeli soldiers and police. Israel responded with tear gas, rubber bullets, and live ammunition. The first intifada ended in 1993, when Israel and the PLO signed the first of two agreements called the Oslo accords.

In 1988, the PLO recognized Israel's right to exist. It also declared its readiness to negotiate with Israel for peace in return for the creation of an independent Palestinian state. In addition, it declared it would no longer use violence against Israel. But some PLO members continued to attack Israeli targets.

The second intifada was more violent. Palestinians carried out many attacks, including suicide bombings, against Israeli soldiers and civilians. Israel repeatedly bombed the West Bank and Gaza Strip, and reoccupied areas in the territories that it had vacated in the mid-1990's as part of the Oslo accords. The second intifada ended after Israel pulled out of the Gaza Strip in 2005. Violence by both sides killed hundreds of Israelis and thousands of Palestinians.

In 1991, the Soviet Union, long the main foreign supporter of anti-Israeli governments and the Palestine Liberation Organization, was dissolved. The Arabs found themselves with much less international support for their fight against Israel.

In October 1991, peace talks began among Israel, Syria, Lebanon, and a joint Jordanian-Palestinian delegation. Israel's Prime Minister Yitzhak Rabin agreed to limit construction of new Jewish settlements in the occupied territories as a step toward a peace agreement. The PLO was not a participant in these peace talks.

Oslo accords

The Oslo accords are two Middle East peace agreements between Israel and the PLO. The Oslo peace process began in 1993 and produced a number of agreements.

In 1993, Israel and the PLO, aided by Norway, began secret peace talks in or around Oslo, the Norwegian capital. As a result, the PLO and Israel signed an agreement in Washington, D.C., on Sept. 13, 1993. Under the agreement, sometimes called Oslo I, the PLO again stated its recognition of Israel's right to exist. Israel, in turn, recognized the PLO as the representative of the Palestinian people. It also promised to withdraw from part or all of the West Bank and Gaza Strip and consider allowing the creation of a Palestinian state in those lands.

Oslo I is officially known as the Declaration of Principles (DOP). The pact established a framework and timetable for the Middle East peace process. It provided for an interim Palestinian government in the Gaza Strip and the town of Jericho (*JEHR uh koh*) in the West Bank. Palestinians make up the majority of the population in the Gaza Strip and the West Bank, but both territories had been occupied by Israel since the 1967 Arab-Israeli Six-Day War. According to Oslo I, administration of the Gaza Strip and Jericho would pass from the Israeli military to a civilian Palestinian administration in 1994. Eventually, elections were to be held for a Palestinian Legislative Council.

The Palestinian Legislative Council is the lawmaking body of the Palestinian Authority, which became the government of the Palestinian people in much of the Gaza Strip and the West Bank. Palestinians refer to it as the Palestinian National Authority. The Gaza Strip and West Bank, along with Israel, make up the region of Palestine.

The PA controls only parts of the Palestinian territories. Israel maintains full control in some areas, particularly places where Israeli settlers

In 1994, PLO leader Yasir Arafat returned to the Gaza Strip following the 1993 Oslo peace accords giving the Palestinian Authority control of Gaza city and Jericho. Palestinian security forces (above) lead a convoy entering Gaza.

live. Israel also controls many major roads in the territories, as well as sites designated as military areas and nature reserves. In some areas, Israel and the PA share control.

A president, elected by the people, heads the PA. A Legislative Council passes laws. The council consists of 88 elected members, plus the president. The president appoints a prime minister, who shares executive authority with the president. The position of prime minister was created in 2003. The prime minister chooses a cabinet to oversee the functions of various executive departments. The Legislative Council must approve appointments to the office of prime minister and to the cabinet.

Not all Israelis agreed with the peace process, and some protested it. Some opponents argued, for example, that Israel was giving away land that should historically belong to it.

In 1994, as a first step of Oslo I, Israel gave the PLO control of the Gaza Strip and the West Bank city of Jericho. In 1995 and 1996, Israel gave the Palestinians control of most cities and towns of the West Bank.

Oslo II, formally called the Israeli-Palestinian Interim Agreement on the West Bank and the Gaza Strip, expanded on Oslo I. The terms of Oslo II included provisions for the complete withdrawal of Israeli troops from six Israeli-occupied West Bank cities and about 450 towns. It also outlined the partial Israeli withdrawal from the West Bank town of Hebron (*HEE bruhn*). Israel gained control of Hebron in the Arab-Israeli Six-Day War of 1967. In addition, the pact set a timetable for elections for the Palestinian Legislative Council and detailed the powers of that body.

As a result of the Oslo accords, the Israelis withdrew from the Gaza Strip and part of the West Bank by 1996. In January 1996, Palestinians in the Gaza Strip and the Palestinian-controlled areas of the West Bank elected a legislature and a president within the PA to make laws and administer these areas. PLO leader Yasir Arafat was elected the PA president. Most of the people elected to the legislature were members of Fatah, the dominant group in the PLO, one that Arafat led after it had grown within the PLO in the 1960's.

Fatah, also called al-Fatah or Fateh, is the largest group within the PLO. *Fatah* is an Arabic term meaning *victory, conquest,* or *opening.* The name *Fatah* also is derived from the initials—in reverse order—of the Arabic phrase that means *Palestine National Liberation Movement.* Fatah calls for using both violent and political means to achieve an independent Palestinian state in Palestine. Fatah began in the late 1950's as a secret movement of a small number of Palestinians. In 1959,

The Oslo II peace agreement outlined the partial withdrawal of Israeli troops from the West Bank town of Hebron (above). Israel gained control of Hebron during the 1967 Arab-Israeli Six-Day War. Hebron is one of the world's oldest cities. It is mentioned in the Bible's Book of Genesis.

Likud Party leader Benjamin Netanyahu (above) greets supporters at a senior citizens' home while campaigning to become
Israel's prime minister. Netanyahu served as prime minister from
1996 to 1999. He began serving a second term in 2009.

Fatah started publishing a magazine that promoted taking up arms to
free Palestine from Israeli control. Fatah grew into a centrally controlled
organization.

Jordan signed a peace treaty with Israel in 1994. Israel then continued to
seek a peace treaty with Syria. However, Syrian-Israeli peace discussions
broke down in 1996. Talks resumed in December 1999 but stopped the
next month because of continuing disagreement over the Golan Heights.

Tensions between Israel and the Palestinians grew after the 1996 Israeli elections, which brought in Likud leader Benjamin Netanyahu (*neh tahn YAH hoo*) as prime minister. With Netanyahu in power, the peace process slowed. Netahyahu's first term lasted until 1999, and he began serving a second term in 2009. He has long been critical of the peace agreements between Israel and the PLO. Netanyahu has claimed that the agreements did not include enough provisions for Israel, such as guaranteed security and allowance for its population growth.

Netanyahu, whose first name is sometimes spelled Binyamin, was born in Tel Aviv on Oct. 21, 1949. He served in the Israel Defense Force from 1967 to 1972. He then studied at the Massachusetts Institute of Technology, where he received a master's degree in management in 1976. From 1984 to 1988, he was the Israeli ambassador to the United Nations. He was elected to the Knesset in 1988 and served as deputy minister of foreign affairs from 1988 to 1991. Netanyahu was elected leader of Likud in 1993. He resigned as Likud leader in 1999 after losing his bid for reelection as prime minister. From 2002 to 2003, Netanyahu served as Israel's foreign minister. From 2003 to 2005, he served as Israel's finance minister. In 2005, he was again elected leader of Likud.

In 1996 and 1997, Israel announced plans to expand Israeli settlements in the West Bank and to build new Israeli housing in East Jerusalem. Both decisions met with angry protests from the Palestinians.

In October 1998, Israel and the Palestinians signed another agreement. Under the accord, Israel turned over more land in the West Bank to Palestinian control. Also, because of the agreement, the PLO revised its charter to remove language calling for the destruction of Israel. Many conservative members of the Israeli parliament and in Netanyahu's cabinet opposed the accord. In December 1998, Netanyahu, claiming that the PLO was not fulfilling its security commitments, suspended

Israeli troop withdrawals from the West Bank.

While peace talks stalled under the Netanyahu government, hopes for continuation were renewed after the election of Ehud Barak as Israeli prime minister in 1999. Barak favored renewing the peace process with the Palestinians. He revived talks regarding control of the Gaza Strip and West Bank and other issues.

Barak was born Ehud Brog on Feb. 12, 1942, in a collective community called a *kibbutz* (*kih BOOTS*) on the Mediterranean coast of what is now Israel. (A kibbutz is a type of Jewish community in Israel based on the idea of social and economic equality. Members of a kibbutz share

Ehud Barak favored renewing the peace process with the Palestinians after his election as Israel's prime minister in 1999. Barak (left), leader of Israel's Labor Party, and PLO leader Yasir Arafat (right) met in face-to-face talks in Gaza in July 1997 in an effort to end the Palestinian-Israeli conflict.

ownership of all the kibbutz's means of income production, including land and businesses. Members also own all houses and buildings on kibbutz land in common. The kibbutz provides education, health care, and housing to individual and families.) Barak earned a B.S. degree in physics and mathematics from Hebrew University in Jerusalem in 1968 and an M.S. degree in economic engineering systems from Stanford University in the United States in 1978.

Barak joined the Israeli army in 1959. He changed his name from Brog to Barak when he became an officer. *Barak* means *lightning* in Hebrew. Barak held several positions of command through the years, including army chief of staff from 1991 to 1995. In 1995, he left the army for politics and served first as interior minister and then as foreign minister. He was elected leader of the Labor Party in 1997. In September 1998, Barak and Palestinian leader Yasir Arafat signed a new agreement that revived and expanded on the previous Wye River Memorandum (see below). Israel resumed its troop withdrawals from the West Bank shortly after the agreement was signed. Barak resigned as Labor leader following his defeat in the 2001 election. From 2007 to 2011, he again led the Labor Party. In 2011, he left the party to set up a new party called Atzmaut (Independence). Barak retired from politics in 2013.

Wye River Memorandum

The Wye River Memorandum was a Middle East peace agreement between the Israelis and the Palestinians that was negotiated at the Wye Plantation in the town of Wye, in Maryland. It was signed in Washington, D.C., on Oct. 23, 1998. However, most of the provisions of the memorandum were never carried out.

The terms of the Wye agreement included a provision that called for Israel to withdraw its troops from 13 percent of the West Bank. Palestinians make up most of the population of the West Bank, but the territory had been occupied by Israel since the 1967 Six-Day War. Under the Wye accord, the Palestinians agreed to crack down on Islamic terrorists and to remove provisions in the PLO charter that called for Israel's destruction. The pact also provided for the opening of an international airport in the Gaza Strip, a territory administered by the Palestinians but occupied by the Israelis from 1967 to 1994.

Prime Minister Benjamin Netanyahu signed the Wye agreement for the Israelis, and Palestinian leader Yasir Arafat signed for the Palestinians. Netanyahu, leader of the conservative Likud party, had opposed earlier Arab-Israeli peace deals. Since 1997, peace talks had stalled, partly because Netanyahu had refused to carry out further troop withdrawals from the West Bank unless the Palestinians did more to stop terrorism. Many conservatives in the Israeli parliament and in Netanyahu's Cabinet opposed the Wye accord. In December

PLO leader Yasir Arafat (left) and Israeli Prime Minister Benjamin Netanyahu shake hands, as Jordan's King Hussein (second from left) and U.S. President Bill Clinton stand by after nine days of peace talks in 1998 at Wye Plantation in Maryland. The signing of the Wye River Memorandum took place at the White House.

In 2002, Israel reoccupied most West Bank cities and began constructing a barrier system to separate most of the West Bank from Israel. Palestinians are shown here walking past the cement barrier at a checkpoint crossing just south of the West Bank city of Ramallah.

1998, Netanyahu accused the Palestinians of failing to keep the security commitments called for in the Wye accord, and he suspended troop withdrawals from the West Bank. That same month, the Israeli parliament voted to dissolve itself and scheduled new elections.

In May 1999, Labor Party leader Ehud Barak was elected as prime minister, promising renewed peace talks. On September 4, Barak and Arafat signed a new agreement in Sharm el-Sheikh (*shahrm ehl shayk*) (also spelled Sharm ash Shaykh), Egypt. This agreement, officially

known as the Sharm el-Sheikh Memorandum, is often referred to as Wye Two. The accord revived and expanded on the previous Wye River Memorandum. For example, the agreement called for three Israeli withdrawals from the West Bank by late January 2000. It also gave Israel and the PLO a year to negotiate a final peace settlement. Israel resumed its troop withdrawals from the West Bank shortly after the Wye deal was signed.

Peace talks between Israeli and Palestinian leaders continued in 2000.

However, the two sides were unable to agree on certain key issues, particularly those involving the final status of Jerusalem.

In September 2000, Palestinians began a second intifada. They began riots and demonstrations against Israeli security forces. Numerous attacks by Palestinian militias and suicide bombings occurred across Israel, the West Bank, and the Gaza Strip, killing hundreds of Israelis. Israeli forces repeatedly bombed and invaded the West Bank and Gaza Strip, killing thousands of Palestinians and demolishing hundreds of houses.

In October, Prime Minister Ehud Barak suspended the peace talks following several weeks of violent clashes between Palestinian demonstrators and Israeli security forces.

In 2001, Israel closed the Gaza Strip airport that had opened under the terms of the Wye River Memorandum. In 2002, Israel reoccupied most West Bank cities. That same year, Israel began constructing a barrier designed to separate most of the West Bank from Israel.

In November 2001, bowing to pressure from opposition parties, Barak agreed to hold a new election for prime minister. He lost the February 2001 election to Ariel Sharon, the leader of the conservative Likud party. Like Netanyahu, Sharon was critical of the Oslo accords.

In 2003, diplomats from the United States, Russia, the European Union, and the United Nations proposed a peace plan known as the "roadmap." Israeli and Palestinian leaders resumed negotiations under this plan, but the negotiations soon broke down. Palestinian attacks and Israeli military strikes continued.

In early 2005, Israeli Prime Minister Sharon and Palestinian leader Mahmoud Abbas (1935-   ) met in Egypt and declared an Israeli-Palestinian truce. However, some violence continued between the two sides.

In 2004, Sharon had announced a plan to remove all Jewish settlements and Israeli troops from the Gaza Strip by the end of 2005. On Aug. 15, 2005, the Israeli government began the evacuation of all Jewish settlers from the Gaza Strip and four West Bank settlements. Many settlers protested the evacuation, and Israeli troops forcibly removed them. The settler evacuation was completed on August 23. The last Israeli troops evacuated on September 20. There are still about 120 Jewish settlements in the West Bank.

Radical resistance

In June 2006, Palestinian militant groups captured an Israeli soldier. The groups demanded Israel release Palestinian prisoners in exchange for the soldier. Fighting between the two sides increased. Israel bombed parts of the Gaza Strip, and militants fired rockets into Israel. Israeli troops entered the Gaza Strip, and fighting there killed over 300 people. In November, both sides agreed to a cease-fire.

In July 2006, Hezbollah (*hehz buh LAH*), a radical Islamic group in Lebanon, captured two Israeli soldiers near the border of Lebanon and Israel. In response, Israel began bombing Lebanon. Israel blamed the Lebanese government for not disarming Hezbollah. Hezbollah fired missiles into northern Israel. In August, Israel and Lebanon accepted a cease-fire agreement drafted by the United Nations Security Council. The conflict caused over 1,000 Lebanese and Israeli deaths. Hezbollah was formed partly as a response to Israel's invasion of Lebanon in 1982. After the invasion, Israeli forces continued to occupy southern Lebanon. Hezbollah guerrillas battled Israeli forces there throughout the 1980's and 1990's.

In December 2008, Israel launched air attacks on targets in the Gaza Strip, stating that the airstrikes were in response to rocket attacks from militants of the radical Palestinian group Hamas. In early January 2009,

Hamas

Hamas (*hah MAHS*) is a radical Palestinian organization and political party. It believes that all of historic Palestine — Israel, the Israeli-occupied West Bank, and the Gaza Strip—rightfully belongs to the Palestinian people. Hamas does not accept Israel and wants to create an Islamic state in Palestine. Hamas opposes the Oslo accords, the agreements signed in the 1990's that sought to establish peace between Israel and the Palestinians. Hamas has carried out terrorist acts against Israeli civilians. The group also distributes food, operates schools and clinics, and provides other services to Palestinians in the West Bank and the Gaza Strip. *Hamas* is an Arabic term that means *enthusiasm* or *zeal*. The name also is derived from the initials of the Arabic phrase that means *Islamic Resistance Movement*.

Hamas was founded in 1987 at the start of a Palestinian *intifada* (uprising) against Israel's occupation of Palestinian areas. Hamas grew out of the Palestinian branch of the Muslim Brotherhood, a religious and political movement founded in Egypt in 1928. Hamas organized a military wing, the Izz al-Din al-Qassam Brigades, to carry out attacks against Israeli targets. Attacks have included the launching of homemade missiles into Israel, ambushes of Israeli troops, and suicide bombings. In 2004, Israel assassinated Hamas's founder and spiritual leader, Sheik Ahmad Yassin (*shayk AH mahd yah SEEN*) (1937-2004), and one of its top leaders, Abdel Aziz al-Rantisi (*AHB duhl ah ZEEZ ahl rahn TEE see*) (1947-2004).

Hamas originally opposed the Palestinian Authority (PA), the governing body created under the Oslo accords. However, in 2006,

Hamas ran as a political party in Palestinian Authority elections and won control of the government. The United States, the European Union, and other countries boycotted the Hamas government, leading to financial and humanitarian hardship in the Palestinian territories.

Hamas has also had strained relations with the Palestinian Authority president, Mahmoud Abbas of the Fatah party, and with the Palestine Liberation Organization. Tension between Fatah and Hamas has at times led to violence among Palestinians.

In June 2007, Hamas seized control of the Gaza Strip by force. Violence between Palestinians and Israeli forces in Gaza—most notably in 2008, 2009, and 2012—killed hundreds of people, most of them Palestinian.

In 2014, after years of negotiations, Hamas and Fatah announced a reconciliation deal. A combined Palestinian government was formed in June. In July, Israeli soldiers entered Gaza after a sharp increase in cross-border violence. Over the next several weeks, more than 2,000 Palestinians were killed, as were dozens of Israelis.

In October 2015, violence again flared up in the occupied territories and has continued since then, resulting in the deaths of dozens of people, mostly Palestinians.

Hezbollah militants bombed the U.S. Embassy building in Beirut, Lebanon (shown above), in 1983, killing 80 people.

Israel began sending troops into the Gaza Strip. The fighting caused more than 1,300 deaths, almost all of them Palestinians, and wounded thousands more. On January 17, Israel declared a cease-fire. Hamas declared a cease-fire the next day, though some fighting continued.

In November 2012, violence in Gaza erupted again as Hamas rocket attacks provoked Israeli naval and air strikes. In roughly one week, about 170 people were killed, all but 6 of them Palestinian.

In July 2014, Israeli soldiers again entered Gaza after a sharp increase in cross-border violence. Over the next several weeks, more than 2,000 Palestinians were killed, as were dozens of Israelis. Dozens of people, mostly Palestinians, have been killed in a new wave of violence that began in the occupied Palestinian territories in 2015.

Hezbollah

Hezbollah (*HEHZ buh LAH*) is a radical Islamic group in Lebanon. The name is also spelled Hizballah, Hizbollah, or Hizbullah. Hezbollah is an Arabic term meaning Party of God. Hezbollah is associated with the Shī`ah branch of Islam. Hezbollah has carried out many terrorist acts against Israeli and Western targets. It also participates in Lebanese politics and provides education, health care, and other services for Shī`ites in Lebanon.

Hezbollah draws its inspiration from the 1979 revolution in Iran that turned that country into an Islamic republic. Hezbollah has called for a similar revolution in Lebanon. Hezbollah also opposes Israel and calls for an end to Israeli occupation of Palestinian areas. Iran provides Hezbollah with financial aid, training, weapons, and political support. Syria—which had troops in Lebanon from 1976 to 2005—also supports Hezbollah.

Hezbollah was formed in 1982 when a group of radical Shī`ites broke away from Lebanon's main Shī`ah political party. The creation of Hezbollah was partly a response to Israel's invasion of Lebanon in 1982. After the invasion, Israeli forces continued to occupy southern Lebanon. Hezbollah guerrillas battled Israeli forces in the area throughout the 1980's and 1990's. In 2000, Israeli troops withdrew from the area.

Hezbollah has engaged in terrorism since its formation. In 1983 and 1984, Hezbollah militants blew up the United States embassy and annex in the Lebanese capital of Beirut, killing about 80 people. In 1983, Hezbollah suicide bombers attacked the U.S. Marine and French Foreign Legion headquarters in Beirut, killing about 300 soldiers. From 1984 to 1992, Hezbollah held several Americans and Europeans as hostages.

FIND OUT MORE!

Black, Ian. *Enemies and Neighbors: A New History of the Israel-Palestine Conflict.* Grove Pr., 2017.

Cohn-Sherbok, Dan, and El Alami, D. S. *The Palestine-Israeli Conflict: A Beginner's Guide.* Rev. ed. Oneworld, 2015.

Roberts, Priscilla M. *Arab-Israeli Conflict: A Documentary and Reference Guide.* Greenwood, 2017.

United Nations: The Question of Palestine. https://www.un.org/unispal/

ACKNOWLEDGMENTS

Cover: © VanderWolf Images/Shutterstock; © ZouZou/Shutterstock; © Ilia Yefimovich, Getty Images; © Vic Hinterlang, iStockphoto; Central Intelligence Agency
4 Public Domain
6 Public Domain (Israeli Pikiwiki project)
8 © Everett Historical/Shutterstock
11 © Culture Club/Getty Images
12-15 Public Domain
17 Library of Congress
18-19 Israel Government Press Office (licensed under CC BY-SA 3.0); © Everett Historical/Shutterstock
20 Israel Government Press Office
22 *Market at Jaffa* (1877), oil on canvas by Gustav Bauernfeind
25 WORLD BOOK map
26-27 © ChameleonsEye/Shutterstock
31 © Shutterstock
32 WORLD BOOK map
35 Library of Congress
36 WORLD BOOK map
38 Flag Research Center
40 U.S. Army Corps of Engineers
42-43 © Mohamed Elsayyed, Shutterstock
44 © Bettmann/Getty Images
47 WORLD BOOK map
48 © Nagel Photography/Shutterstock

51 National Archives
54 Israel Government Press Office (licensed under CC BY-SA 3.0)
56-57 Stevan Kragujević (licensed under CC BY-SA 3.0); Public Domain
58 WORLD BOOK map
59 Public Domain
61 © Everett Historical/Shutterstock
63 WORLD BOOK map
65 © AFP/Getty Images
66 © David Lees, The LIFE Images Collection/Getty Images
69-73 Israel Government Press Office (licensed under CC BY-SA 4.0)
71 WORLD BOOK map
75 Central Intelligence Agency
76 WORLD BOOK map
78 Public Domain
81 © Mark Reinstein, Shutterstock
82 © Mario De Biasi, Mondadori Portfolio/Getty Images
84 National Archives
87 © ChameleonsEye/Shutterstock
89-91 Israel Government Press Office (licensed under CC BY-SA 4.0)
95 Palestinian Press Office
97 Kremlin.ru (licensed under CC BY 4.0)
99 Public Domain
100 Israel Government Press Office (licensed under CC BY-SA 3.0)

102 National Archives
105 © David Rubinger, The LIFE Images Collection/Getty Images
106 © Thomas Coex, AFP/Getty Images
109 © Patrick Baz, AFP/Getty Images
111 © Mtsyri/Shutterstock
112 © David Rubinger, The LIFE Images Collection/Getty Images
114 © Waizmann/ullstein bild/Getty Images
116-117 The White House
118-119 © Abbas Momani, AFP/Getty Images
124 U.S. Army